The Soul

Revisioning Philosophy

David Appelbaum
General Editor

Vol. 15

PETER LANG
New York • Washington, D.C./Baltimore • San Francisco
Bern • Frankfurt am Main • Berlin • Vienna • Paris

Adrian Kuzminski

The Soul

PETER LANG
New York • Washington, D.C./Baltimore • San Francisco
Bern • Frankfurt am Main • Berlin • Vienna • Paris

Library of Congress Cataloging-in-Publication Data

Kuzminski, Adrian.
   The soul / Adrian Kuzminski.
     p.   cm. — (Revisioning philosophy; vol. 15)
   Includes bibliographical references and index.
   1. Soul. I. Title. II. Series.
BD421.K89   1994   128'.1—dc20   93-8720
ISBN 0-8204-2279-7   CIP
ISSN 0899-9937

Die Deutsche Bibliothek-CIP-Einheitsaufnahme

Kuzminski, Adrian:
The soul / Adrian Kuzminski. - New York; San Francisco; Bern; Baltimore;
Frankfurt am Main; Berlin; Wien; Paris: Lang, 1994
  (Revisioning philosophy; Vol. 15)
  ISBN 0-8204-2279-7
NE: GT

The paper in this book meets the guidelines for permanence and durability of
the Committee on Production Guidelines for Book Longevity of the
Council on Library Resources.

© Peter Lang Publishing, Inc., New York 1994

All rights reserved.
Reprint or reproduction, even partially, in all forms such as microfilm,
xerography, microfiche, microcard, offset strictly prohibited.

Printed in the United States of America.

To my mother

Janina Kuzminski

Contents

Preface ix

Chapter 1   Perception 1

Chapter 2   Representation and Contrast 21

Chapter 3   Sensations and Thoughts 43

Chapter 4   Solipsism and Behaviorism 63

Chapter 5   Signs 87

Chapter 6   Language 109

Chapter 7   The Soul 129

Bibliography 145

Index 155

Preface

A book on the soul will strike some as quaint, if not naively misguided. The soul, after all, has long been relegated by secular thinkers, including most philosophers, to the lumber room of history. Among the religiously inclined, for whom it has remained meaningful, it is usually uncritically presupposed. Yet I propose to revive the notion of the soul as the central item in our understanding of experience, giving it an importance it has not had in philosophy perhaps since Socrates. To this end, I undertake a fundamental philosophical exposition of experience. I adopt an axiomatic approach stipulating two major intuitions: the first concerning the nature of perception, and the second concerning the nature of the soul.

My methods are by current standards unorthodox. I argue by stipulation, laying down assumptions and drawing out consequences. Most philosophers today are professionals. By training and necessity they proceed historically, not stipulatively. If the literature of the tradition were always adequate to our intuitions, the historical-academic method could justly claim a monopoly over how to do philosophy. But any effort to do justice to intuitions not directly or in essentials anticipated in the tradition cannot proceed historically. It must rather unwind from itself in its own idiom. Philosophers as diverse as Plato, Descartes, Spinoza, Berkeley, Nietzsche, and Wittgenstein argued mainly by stipulation. They put forth more or less original hypotheses (sometimes one, sometimes many) and developed their implications, with relatively little discussion 'of the literature.'

I write therefore not as an academic scholar, commenting primarily on the texts of others, but as a independent philosopher bending the English language as best I can to the service of my intuitions. If the reader is to gain much from what follows, I must provisionally be granted my pretension. Allow me, with patience, to unfold my hypotheses and their implications, and let these finally be judged in the light of your own experience.

My bibliography nonetheless acknowledges the vast debt I owe to the literature, to those who have written about the soul, consciousness, and truth. I am indebted to some works in that literature more than others, and among these particularly are the works of Berkeley and Wittgenstein. It was through Berkeley—on whom I wrote a doctoral dissertation—that I realized my perceptions were somehow part of me, but that I was not myself a perception. And it was later, through reading and teaching Wittgenstein, that I realized that perception *is* representation.

This is how I came to read Wittgenstein in a Berkeleian context. In Berkeley's metaphysics, perceptions are immediate objects of consciousness, so immediate as not to require a body to be perceived. I follow Berkeley in rejecting the assumption that perceptions arise only upon or within the surface of a physical body, that a perception is necessarily a sensation triggered by neural stimulation. I hold the Berkeleian view that sensation is merely one sort of perception, that there are perceptions other than sensations, and that there are intuitions other than perceptions. I read Wittgenstein's 'facts' as perceptions in this larger sense—I identify representation with perception —and I understand what Wittgenstein called the 'ineffable' in the Berkeleian sense as intuition beyond perception.

*

In this work I begin with the hypothesis that perception is representation. I argue that perceptions are those objects of awareness that are distinguished by mutual comparison. These include our thoughts and sensations, which constitute what we normally call objects and events: non-physical and physical, private and public. I attempt to show that thoughts and sensations constitute objects and events by standing to one another as representations and contrasts, that is, as variously the same, similar, or different vis-a-vis one another. I conclude that thoughts do not occur in the body, that sensations do not occur in the mind, but that thoughts and sensations, which together constitute us as persons, somehow occur for us as souls.

Thoughts and sensations, however, are easily misunderstood and often confused with one another. I argue that these confusions, which I call solipsism and behaviorism, sustain our philosophical and religious dogmatisms by encouraging the mis-identification of self with thought (mind) or sensation (body). It is this mis-identification of self with mind or body which denies the soul and represses any understanding of who we are. By rejecting the dogmatic claims of solipsistic religiosity and behavioristic ideology, I open the way to my second philosophical intuition: an appreciation of the actual self, of the soul. Along the way—in chapters five and six—I explore the implications of perception and its solipsistic and behavioristic distortions with regard to signification and language.

I then turn towards the soul, which reveals itself as a singular unfolding presence. The 'soul' goes back into deep prehistory as a name for some kind of enduring self distinct from the body. I affirm this, and argue additionally that the soul is as distinct from the mind as it is from the body. The soul is no more a mental thing than it is a physical thing, no more a thought than a sensation. Although we can both think and sense perceptions, we cannot think or sense our souls. The existence of the soul is independent of our thoughts and sensations, of the persons we in fact happen to be.

I argue for a non-perceptual consciousness of soul and its major aspects: emotion and will. The soul, my second philosophical intuition, arises out of the first, that perception is representation. To come to consciousness of the soul is to recognize the possibility of liberation from our normal enthrallment to perception. It is also to recognize that others like us are souls, that we do not swim alone in the perceptual sea. The mutual recognition of souls promises to be a new basis for individual and social transcendence. To continue to see self and others as bodies or minds is, I argue, to perpetuate the cycles of our deepest regressions and alienations, the fears and resentments that erupt into aggression and violence against people and nature.

*

Most of this work was thought out in relative solitude over twenty years and more, so I have few acknowledgments. My early and sometimes unwitting teachers in philosophy were William Kennick, George Kateb, Hayden V. White, Marvin Bram, Norman O. Brown, R. J. Kaufmann, Lewis White Beck, Colin Murray Turbayne, and A. A. Luce. Advice and degrees of encouragement and assistance at different stages of this work, in different forms, came from Sylvia Tesh, Robert C. Neville, Paul Weiss, and David Appelbaum. I owe my wife T'nette an incalculable debt. Richard T. Vann and the editorial board of *History and Theory* were kind enough to publish some earlier papers of mine on related themes, and I will always be grateful for the philosophical discussions Glenn Kim and I carried on in Honolulu, now so many years ago.

Adrian Kuzminski,
Honolulu, Hawaii, and
Fly Creek, New York
1973-1993

CHAPTER ONE

Perception

Reality is whatever exists; any reality, anything that exists, is a fact. Our reality is whatever exists for us; it is our experience of the facts.

Some facts are ubiquitous; they consistently accompany other facts.

Perceptions and souls are ubiquitous facts, at least in our experience; they consistently accompany one another.

For us, there are no perceptions without souls, and no souls without perceptions.

If there are further ubiquitous facts, they are not (yet) facts for us.

*

Perceptions are complex, reactive, unconscious facts. Souls are simple, proactive, conscious facts.

The complexity of perceptions allows for their display and comparison, but the simplicity of souls makes impossible any display or comparison of souls. We can display our perceptions, but not our souls.

Reactive perceptions require a stimulus to act, but proactive souls themselves have the capacity to initiate action.

Perceptions are entirely unconscious facts; but souls are facts conscious both of themselves and of perceptions.

Human beings are souls whose perceptions include sensations and thoughts.

I begin with perception, and end with the soul.

*

A perception is a complication—a disturbance, an event, an object, a change—vis-a-vis other such complications.

The complexity of perceptions allows them to be displayed—to be the same, similar, or different from one another—thereby providing a standard of mutual comparison.

To specify the comparative features which distinguish perceptions from one another—sameness, similarity, and difference—is to specify the features which perceptions share as perceptions.

Only those features which perceptions share as perceptions—sameness, similarity, and difference—make it possible for any perception to be distinguished as a perception.

The other features which perceptions share as perceptions—reactiveness and unconsciousness—have no comparative value among perceptions.

*

Any perception displays the complexity of differentiation. Perceptions appear always complex, never simple.

There is no single or simple perception. Every perception is the product of its constituent perceptions, and is itself a constituent of further perceptions. Every perception is in this way a combination of perceptions.

Perception

Combined perceptions constitute a nesting fabric, one perception always within another. The nesting of perceptions, which makes possible their comparison, can be summarized as follows:

1) All perceptions have perceptions as parts; and all perceptions are parts of perceptions.

2) Any perception, since it has parts, is a whole; and any perception, since it contributes to some whole, is a part.

3) All perceptions are wholes with respect to their parts, and parts with respect to their wholes.

4) Any perception is at once a whole and a part.

*

If there were perceptions which had no perceptions as parts, which were not the products of perceptual combination, they would be elementary perceptions. But since all perceptions must have perceptions as parts, there can be no elementary perceptions.

If there were perceptions which had all perceptions as their parts, which were themselves the product of all perceptual combination, they would be absolute perceptions. But since all perceptions must be parts of perceptions, there can be no absolute perceptions.

To admit elementary perceptions or absolute perceptions would be to admit absurd perceptions, perceptions which could not be perceptions.

A perception which ceased to have parts, or which ceased to be part of a whole, would cease to be a perception. It could not be distinguished as a perception. Anything which has no perceptions as parts, or which is part of no perception, is not a perception.

If I cannot distinguish a perception into parts, I cannot distinguish that perception at all. Even the smallest perception, say a point . , must have parts that I can make out if I am to establish it as a point.

If I cannot distinguish a perception as a part, I cannot distinguish that perception at all. Even the most inclusive perception can be a perception for me only if I can also see that it is a part of some further perception.

No particles isolated in micro-physics can be elementary perceptions. For any particle must, if it is a perception, itself have perceptions as parts; and so on for those parts in turn, and for their parts, etc.

Neither can the macro-physical universe as a whole (the cosmos) be an absolute perception, nor can language, nor history, nor culture, or any other purportedly exhaustive whole. For all these must, if they are perceptions, themselves be parts of further perceptions; and so on for those perceptions in turn, and for the perceptions of which they are parts, etc.

*

Relations among perceptions are what make them parts of a common whole, a larger perception. Alternative relations among perceptions make them, in different ways, parts of different wholes, of different perceptions.

Consider a set of toy blocks stacked neatly on the floor as a perception. Those same blocks when scattered on the floor constitute another perception. The indefinite number of further ways those blocks can be related to one another constitute an indefinite number of further perceptions.

A perception can never be distinguished in itself, but only in terms of other perceptions: those which are its parts, those with which it combines as a part, and those with which it is compared.

A perception is distinguished as a part by the external relations into which it enters as a whole with other perceptions. A perception is distinguished as a whole by its internal relations, by the relations collectively displayed by the perceptions which are its parts.

The wholeness of a perception is the network of relations its parts display with regard to one another: these are its **internal relations**.

The partness of a perception is the network of relations it effects with other perceptions so as to constitute some further whole, some further perception: these are its **external relations.**

The internal relations displayed by a perception constitute the **forms** of that perception; the wholeness of a perception is its forms.

The external relations effected by a perception constitute, at least in part, the forms of some larger perception. The partness of a perception is its role (minimally as a point) in displaying the forms of some perception of which it is a part.

To display a perception as a whole is to specify that perception. It is to locate its parts with respect to one another. To display a perception as a part is to locate that perception. It is to specify the whole of which it is a part.

This is not to say that the partness of a perception does not help to make it the perception that it is. It is to say that a perception can display itself only as a whole, and never as a part.

*

To specify a perception is to unfold it, to spread it out into a display of its parts, into a field. To locate a perception is to fold it up, to condense it into a point, as if it had no parts, and relate it to other perception-points. Perception-fields are perceptions taken as wholes. Perception-points are perceptions taken as parts.

The two-sidedness of perceptions—their wholeness and partness—is expressed in quantum physics as Bohr's principle of complementarity. Complementarity holds that a perception can be a field or a point, but that at any given moment it can be only one or the other.

A perception-field constitutes a space, with its mass dispersed over that space, subject (in sensation) to the classical field-equations. A perception-point constitutes a particle, with its mass concentrated at a single point, subject (in sensation) to the classical laws of motion.

In subatomic micro-physics, where the minimum necessary quantum of energy for gross objects (indicated by Planck's constant) is lacking, objects can exist only momentarily. We are allowed at best only one perception of such an object. We can choose to observe either its partness or its wholeness, its location or its specificity, but not both.

This is Heisenberg's principle of indeterminacy. Grosser objects (where Planck's constant is insignificant) have sufficient energy to provide for a sustained perception. The gross object can be reobserved, often very rapidly, so that both its partness and its wholeness, its location and its specificity, can be determined.

But even on the gross material level complementarity is maintained by the need to carry out separate and successive (even if virtually instantaneous) determinations, one for wholeness and one for partness.

Modern atomic physics has shown that what we call material perceptions (or sensations) are packages of bound energy, in which gravitational, electromagnetic, nuclear, and sub-nuclear forces are variously balanced in repetitive patterns subject to the limitations of quantum physics. The balanced stability of these bound perceptions is what gives our material perceptions their resistance, their relative impenetrability.

In physics, there is no dichotomy between matter and energy. Matter is but a family of perceptual forms, a type of energy, bound rather than expansive. Modern physics tells us that energy can be bound into matter, and that matter can be unbound into energy.

*

In addition to the world of sensation addressed in the physical sciences, we have other perceptions we call thoughts. I think thoughts just as I see sights, hear sounds, feel touches, smell aromas, and taste flavors.

Thoughts are not concepts (which belong to the world of sensation), but concrete images in what we call memory and imagination.

Perception

The world of thought stands in contrast to the world of sensation. Thoughts defy the laws of physics, freely violating the constraints of space, time, and matter which hold in the world of sensation.

In thought I can be in two places at once, defy gravity, leave my body, and do many other things I can never do in sensation.

Thoughts are remarkable in their fluidity and ease, very unlike the fixity and resistance of physical perceptions. We compare thoughts much more rapidly and freely than we compare sensations (sights, sounds, and the rest).

But thought-perceptions, like physical-perceptions, are indubitably just the perceptions that they are. Any thought perception I absorb is simply and wholly just the perception that it is.

The world of thought appears unconnected to, but parallel with, the world of sensation. Thoughts appear to constitute a perceptual family distinct from, but similar to, the perceptual family of sensations.

The temptation in sensation is to abstract recurring regularities, setting them up as independent criteria, as non-sensible forms into which the content of chaotic sensibility is to be poured and shaped: the ideological impulse.

The parallel temptation in thought is to capture and elevate certain compelling images, to reinforce their aesthetic power and impose them as independent criteria upon the rest of experience: the religious impulse.

The difference between thoughts and sensations testifies to a deeper complexity in our perceptual spectrum, and stands as a warning against the error of trying to reduce thoughts to sensations, or sensations to thoughts.

Thoughts and sensations, however they differ, both remain perceptions. Each thought and perception is a part and whole nesting complex, with its internal and external relations.

*

The internal relations of a perception are its own forms displayed by its own parts. The external relations of any perception are the forms of the perception of which it is a part, and which it helps to display.

The forms of my house, for example, comprise the complex network of internal relations displayed by the parts that make it up in just the way that they do so: namely, the roof, the sides, the foundations, as well as the windows, the siding, the porch, not to mention everything within the house, the plumbing, the furniture, the appliances, and so forth, all assembled together just as they are.

The forms of my dog, (a labrador retriever) are displayed in just the same way: his various parts—his short black hair, his floppy ears, his barrel chest, his mournful eyes, his boxy head, and so on. In each case, the parts display the forms that they display by being arranged together in just the way that they are arranged.

The forms, or internal relations, of a perception are not in themselves perceptions. They are configurations of perceptions. The forms of a perception are displayed by its parts, which are themselves perceptions. There can be no configuration of perceptions without perceptions with which to configure. There can be no forms unless there are perceptions related together to display forms.

Neither is the partness of a perception, its locus as a junction of external relations, a perception. Rather its partness is the role that perception plays in one (or another) network of relations with other perceptions so as to constitute a further, inclusive perception. No perception can be a part without there being other perceptions with which it can be a part.

My house, my dog, the memory of my grandmother, or any other specific perception is, as a perception, neither the forms displayed by its parts, nor the partness it exhibits in relation to other perceptions. Rather it is both of these at once. My house is not, as a perception, the forms displayed by its parts (its windows, its roof, its porch, etc.). Nor is it, as a perception, the various relations into which it enters with other perceptions—for instance, as a taxable item, as a potential commodity in the real estate market, as an example of a certain type of architecture, etc.

Neither is my dog, as a perception, the forms displayed by his parts (his eyes, his nose, his floppy ears, etc.). Neither is he, as a perception, the various relations into which he enters with other perceptions—for instance, the dog who runs in the field, the dog who eats camembert cheese, and so on. My house, my dog, or any other specific perception is a perception only insofar as the forms it displays through its parts are also themselves parts of a larger perception.

Although forms (relations) do not in themselves constitute a perception, a perception can display itself only as a whole and never as a part. The wholeness of a perception is displayed only by its content—by its parts in their relations to one another. The whole of a perception is exactly the display of its parts in their relation to one another.

A perception cannot display itself as a part since its partness is not that perception as it is in itself, but rather that perception as it is in conjunction with other perceptions in some more inclusive perception. The partness of a perception is displayed only through the whole of the inclusive perception of which it is a part.

Any specific perception is the specific perception that it is only if the forms it displays—as a whole and as a part—are specifically configured forms, such as the forms of my house, of my dog, of my grandmother, etc. A specific perception is the specific perception that it is because of the specific configuration of its parts and its role as a part in other wholes. The partness and wholeness of a perception is what makes it the specific perception that it is.

*

As I sit in my chair with my feet propped up and look about the room where I write, I see the perceptions in it just as I see them. And if I get up and look more closely, examine those perceptions more thoroughly, move the furniture about, look in drawers, lift the rug, probe the walls, carry out chemical tests, take X-rays, and so on, I encounter new perceptions. All these new perceptions, moreover, confront me as I discover and examine them in just the same direct way as the perceptions I see when I just look about the room.

It is the same with the thoughts that accompany this activity. As I sit and look about the room I am also thinking. I have thought-perceptions, as well as sensation-perceptions, that is, altogether I have thought-perceptions, visual-perceptions, audible-perceptions, tactile-perceptions, taste-perceptions, and smell-perceptions.

The objection arises that our perceptions can be doubted, that they may not be what they appear to be. It may also be objected that the internal and external relations of a perception are seldom, if ever, fully displayed. If these objections are granted, then to find out what a perception really is one must either break it down (analyze it) to uncover its hidden parts, or else contextualize it (synthesize it) to reveal the hidden wholes to which it belongs.

Analysis, on this view, would reveal the fundamental and determining parts of the original perception, and synthesis would reveal its fundamental and determining wholes. Here we encounter again the idea that there are elementary perceptions on the one hand, and absolute perceptions on the other.

Any perception as it is, however, is just those relations that it displays, and no others. Something further is just that, namely, some further perception, which is itself just those relations that it displays, and so on. There are no hidden parts or wholes.

This is not to say that we cannot subject perceptions to analysis and synthesis. Indeed, that is exactly what we do when we determine the further wholeness and partness of perceptions. However, the original perception, before we analyze or synthesize it, is simply the perception that *it* is, and the new perceptions revealed in the processes of analysis and synthesis are just that—new perceptions.

Any process of analysis or synthesis is itself a perception. The original perception and the new perceptions revealed in such a process become, when taken together, simply the parts of that process—the whole of which is the perception they collectively display. Far from being "hidden" in any original perception, new parts are merely further perceptions which accompany the original as parts in a more inclusive perception.

*

There is no distinction between appearance and reality. Appearance is real and reality appears. A perception I take in at a glance is one perception, say, the clock I see on my wall. A closer examination of that perception will reveal a sequence of further perceptions. I may glance at the clock several times. I may get up and observe it from a number of different perspectives. I may take down the clock, dismantle it, and spread its workings out on a table. The workings I discover when I do so were not among the parts of the clock I saw when I first looked at the clock on the wall.

The original clock on the wall is one perception; its analyzed state on the table quite another. However, both the original clock and the analyzed clock are themselves parts in a process which, in this case, begins with my taking the clock off the wall and ends with my separating the last piece of it I care to separate (given my skill in dismantling clocks, my tools, etc.). This process is itself a whole, a perception, one I call "taking a clock apart."

Further, the clock on my wall is a part in the larger perception which is my room. Taking my clock as a part, I can relate it to other clocks, to the sun, the moon, and the stars. I can give it to a friend. I can put it away, hang it elsewhere, destroy it. And so on. In thus altering the situation of my clock, I place it as a part in a variety of different wholes. The original clock remains the same through most of this. It continues to display itself through its parts in each of the different wholes in which it is placed, up to the point where it is itself altered or destroyed.

Placing the clock as a part in any such sequence of wholes is a synthetic process, and such a process is itself a perception, as is any series of such processes. Indeed, the more or less arbitrary series outlined above I call "doing different things with my clock." Although perceptions can be constituted through analysis and synthesis, analysis and synthesis are not the criteria of the perceptions they constitute. Rather, since any analysis or synthesis is itself a perception, it is validated (like any perception) by its own self-display.

*

Perceptions revealed through analysis or synthesis are mediate perceptions. We are conscious of them as a succession of parts. Immediate perceptions are simultaneous. We are conscious of them as a simultaneity of parts.

To the extent to which perceptions are immediate, they are **objects**. To the extent to which perceptions are mediate, they are **events**. Succession is the appearance and disappearance of parts, one after another. Simultaneity is their mutual persistence.

Events introduce change into the perceptual world through the appearance and disappearance of the perceptions that are their parts. Objects introduce permanence into the perceptual world through the persistence of their parts.

If all perceptions were objects, we would have space without time. If all perceptions were events, we would have time without space. But no perceptions are exclusively objects or events. There are no pure perception-objects or pure perception-events.

There is no perception whose parts might not cease to abide. There is no perception whose parts do not to some degree abide. All perceptions are sumultaneous with some perceptions, and successive to others. Perceptions are at once spatial and temporal, at once objects and events.

Some perceptions have many simultaneously abiding parts, and are for most practical purposes objects: a stone, a bar of gold, a kitchen table, etc. Other perceptions have many successively changing parts, and are for most practical purposes events: a nuclear explosion, the French Revolution, etc.

The immediacy or mediacy of a perception is a function of the specific perception that it is. It is a function of the way in which its forms are distributed simultaneously and successively. The immediacy or mediacy of a perception has nothing to do with its relatedness, with the fact that a relation is effected between perceptions.

The course of an ordinary day outdoors—the rising of the sun, its progress through the sky, the changing shadows, the various winds, sounds, clouds, weathers, and textures, the setting of the sun, twilight, the night with its quiets and chills, and so on—all this is as much a perception as anything we can confront more or less at once, such as a musical tone, a geometrical figure, a pain, or the face of a friend. The course of a day, the face of a friend, or indeed any perception at all it just the perception that it is for me. The end of a perception (the edge of a surface, the last page of a book, etc.) is simply its end, whether it be mediate or immediate.

No perception is vague (or indistinct, or unclear, etc.) except by comparison with another perception. A "vague" perception is quite clearly just the vague perception that it is. And no perception is ambiguous except by comparison with another perception. An "ambiguous" perception is quite clearly just the "ambiguous" perception that it is.

If I say that the view out my window on a foggy morning is vague, I can only mean that it is vague by comparison with other mornings, for instance when it is bright and sunny. But what I see on a foggy morning is just as clearly what I see on a foggy morning as what I see on a sunny morning is just as clearly what I see on a sunny morning.

If the following perception is said to be ambiguous —

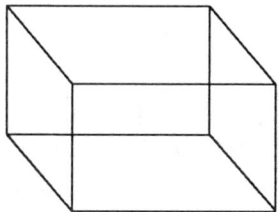

— it can be so only when compared with certain other perceptions, such as these:

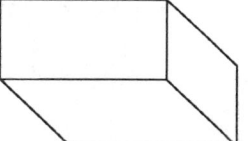 

The first perception is in no way itself ambiguous. It is quite straightforwardly exactly what it is. Ambiguity arises only when comparison is made with the other two. Vagueness, ambiguity, and other such terms mark certain *comparisons* we make among perceptions, not perceptions as such.

Perceptions large or small, temporal or atemporal, physical or mental, and so forth, are exactly what they are, no more and no less. They constitute their own criterion, each of them, and they are in that regard exhaustively self-evident.

Perceptions are just what they are in that they are no more or less than just what they appear to be, than just what is actually differentiated. They are just those parts distinguished as a part of some other whole, which is itself distinguished as a part of some still further whole, and so on.

*

Perceptions are the **same** to the extent to which their forms are the same. Perceptions display the same forms to the extent to which each perception displays a configuration of forms also displayed by other perceptions.

Perceptions are **different** to the extent to which their forms are different. Perceptions display different forms to the extent to which each perception displays a configuration of forms not displayed by other perceptions.

Perceptions are **similar** to the extent to which their forms are similar. Perceptions display similar forms to the extent to which each perception displays a configuration of forms both displayed and not displayed by other perceptions.

Sameness, difference, and similarity (like vagueness and ambiguity) are matters of comparison of perceptions, not of perceptions as such. Unlike vagueness and ambiguity, however, they concern *all* perceptions.

Sameness, similarity, and difference concern perceptions as wholes, not as parts. The role a perception plays as a whole in a larger perception tells us nothing about its internal structure, about the forms it displays as a whole. Perceptions are the same, similar, and different vis-a-vis one another with regard not to the parts they (or their parts) play in larger perceptions but with regard to their wholeness, to their own forms as displayed by their own parts.

*

The possibilities of perceptions displaying the same, similar, or different forms with parts that are are same, similar, or different are as follows:

1) Perceptions can display different forms with the same parts insofar as the same parts can be differently arranged.

2) Perceptions can display the same forms with the same parts insofar as the same parts can be arranged in the same way.

3) Perceptions can display different forms with different parts insofar as different parts can be differently arranged.

4) Perceptions can display the same forms with different parts insofar as different parts can be arranged in the same way.

5) Perceptions can display different forms with similar parts insofar as the same parts can be similarly arranged.

6) Perceptions can display the same forms with similar parts insofar as the similar parts can be differently arranged.

7) Perceptions can display similar forms with the same parts insofar as the same parts can be similarly arranged.

8) Perceptions can display similar forms with different parts insofar as the different parts can be similarly arranged.

9) Perceptions can display similar forms with similar parts insofar as the similar parts can be similarly arranged.

*

To the extent to which perceptions display the same forms, they **represent** one another. To the extent to which perceptions display different forms, they **contrast** with one another. To the extent to which perceptions display similar forms, they both **represent and contrast** with one another.

Representation and contrast are mutually reciprocal. If perception A represents perception A', then perception A' also represents perception A; and if perception X contrasts with perception O, then perception O also contrasts with perception X.

To say that two perceptions represent one another simply because they represent one another is to say that they do so simply because (and insofar as) the relations displayed by the parts of one perception are the same as those displayed by the parts of the other.

And to say that two perceptions contrast with one another simply because they contrast with one another is to say that they do so simply because (and insofar as) the relations displayed by the parts of one perception are different from those displayed by the parts of the other. That representation succeeds or fails is self-evident, insofar as comparison of perceptions is possible.

To hold that perceptions represent one another only insofar as the forms, or internal relationships, they display are the same or similar is not to propose a criterion of representation. It is to take representation as its own criterion. To say that perceptions that represent or contrast with one another do so insofar as they display forms that are the same, similar, or different is to elucidate what is already there. It is to appeal to all the self-evident comparisons of forms displayed by specific perceptions, just as those forms are self-evidently displayed.

To the extent to which a perception represents other perceptions, it is a universal. To the extent to which a perception contrasts with other perceptions, it is a particular.

A perception which represented all other perceptions would be a purely universal perception. A perception which contrasted with all other perceptions would be a purely particular perception. But since all perceptions do not display the same forms, no perception can represent all other perceptions. There is no purely universal perception. And neither do all perceptions contrast with one another; they do not all display different forms.

But there can be perceptions which contrast with all other perceptions. These would be purely particular perceptions. Their pure particularity, however, renders them moot. Sharing no forms with other perceptions, neither simultaneously nor successively, they cannot be represented.

Error concerns not perceptions as such, but the comparison of perceptions. Even though perceptions are indubitably what they are, often we are not in a position to establish for ourselves that one perception is the same, similar, or different from another. The actual comparison of perceptions that would allow us to appreciate the obvious may be second-hand, remote, inconvenient, impossible, or otherwise compromised.

Similarity also introduces uncertainty, even when actual comparison of perceptions can be made, since comparative judgments of similarity are necessarily vague and imprecise. In such situations we can make only presumed comparisons, and inevitably some of these turn out to be wrong.

The truth of a perception is its degree of sameness vis-a-vis another perception. Its falsehood is its degree of difference vis-a-vis another perception. A perception is completely true of another perception if it is wholly identical with it. It is false if it is no more than contingent with it. Sameness is complete truth. Similarity is partial truth and partial falsehood. Difference is complete falsehood.

Perceptions are not true or false in themselves, but only by representational comparison with other perceptions. The existence of a perception—its being, its facticity—is not its truth. Nor is the non-existence of a perception its falsehood. Perceptions as such are neither true nor false. They simply exist.

Difference is not nothing. It is a comparison of non-identical perceptions. Nor is sameness something. It is a comparison of identical perceptions. Nothing is the absence of perceptions, not the absence of sameness. Something is the presence of perceptions, not not the presence of sameness. A potential perception is merely the representation of a perception (in its absence) by another perception.

*

Any perception is related to some (but not all) other perceptions. But perceptions do not represent one another because they are related to one another. Nor do perceptions contrast with one another because they are not related to one another.

Perceptions are related to one another if they are parts of the same whole, but they do not have to be parts of the same whole in order to represent one another. Nor do they have to be parts of different wholes to contrast with one another.

To the extent to which two perceptions, for example,

represent one another, as these do, they do not do so because they are related, that is, because they are parts of the same whole (even if, as here on this page, they are). Rather these (or any other) perceptions represent one another (if they do so) simply because they represent one another.

To the extent to which both these visual bull perceptions contrast with a further perception (say one I cannot visualize, such as the tone of Middle C), they do not do so because they are unrelated, that is, because they are parts of different wholes (even if, other than here,

Perception 19

they usually are). Rather they contrast with one another simply because they contrast with one another.

Since there are perceptions whose parts are perceptions which represent one another, it might seem that the forms of such inclusive perceptions display representation itself. Since perceptions which represent one another can be related together in the larger perception they constitute, it seems plausible to believe that the forms of the larger perception are the forms of their own representation of one another, that is, that there are forms of representation.

For example, if I take a photograph of someone, that photograph and the person photographed represent one another to the extent to which they display the same forms. If I take another photograph which includes the first photograph and the person originally photographed, then the second photograph, in bringing together the original photograph and the person originally photographed, displays that they represent one another.

However, even though a perception whose parts themselves represent one another displays certain relations between those parts, it remains that those relations have nothing to do with whether or not the parts represent one another. We can relate together perceptions which represent one another. But we can just as well relate together perceptions which contrast with one another. Representation cannot be understood as a matter of such relations.

The second photograph cannot photograph how it is that the person photographed and the first photograph of that person succeed in representing one another. It only makes it conveniently obvious that they do so *if* they do so. It only brings out that they correspond in certain ways *if* they do so. It shows nothing about how it is that, even when they do so correspond, they also happen to represent one another.

It is because I can relate perceptions which represent one another into more inclusive perceptions, which can themselves be represented by other perceptions, that I am tempted to conclude that I can represent representation itself. But it cannot be done. Perceptions can only represent (or contrast with) one another, and whether or not they do so is entirely a matter of the specific configurations of forms they display, of their respective internal relations.

Whether or not perceptions display the same, similar, or different forms has nothing to do with whether or not they stand in some relation to one another. Representation and contrast depend on the configuration of the internal relations displayed by perceptions. But how those perceptions themselves stand related to one another has no bearing on how, or whether or not, they represent or contrast with one another.

Only perceptions can be represented and contrasted with one another. Anything that is not a perception (such as my soul) cannot be represented or contrasted in any way. My consciousness of non-perceptions is a non-representational consciousness.

CHAPTER TWO

Representation and Contrast

Representation and contrast are the heart of perception. To be perceived is to be represented and contrasted with other perceptions as the same, similar, or different.

Since perceptions display the same, similar, or different forms using the same, similar, or different parts, the following modes of representation and contrast emerge. These constitute the logic of representation and contrast:

1) Insofar as perceptions display the same forms using the same parts, they are **identical** to one another.

2) Insofar as perceptions display the same forms using similar parts, they are **replicas** of one another.

3) Insofar as perceptions display the same forms using different parts, they are **pictures** of one another.

4) Insofar as perceptions display similar forms using the same parts, they are **varieties** of one another.

5) Insofar as perceptions display similar forms using similar parts, they are **kinds** of one another.

6) Insofar as perceptions display similar forms using different parts, they are **analogs** of one another.

7) Insofar as perceptions display different forms using the same parts, they are **functions** of one another.

8) Insofar as perceptions display different forms using similar parts, they are **homologs** of one another.

9) Insofar as perceptions display different forms using different parts, they are **contingent** to one another.

These modes of representation and contrast can be summarized as follows:

	SAME FORMS	SIMILAR FORMS	DIFFERENT FORMS
SAME PARTS	identities	varieties	functions
SIMILAR PARTS	replicas	kinds	homologs
DIFFERENT PARTS	pictures	analogs	contingencies

Identities are perceptions that are wholly the same. Contingencies are perceptions that are wholly different. Kinds are perceptions that are wholly similar.

Pictures display sameness in terms of difference. Functions display difference in terms of sameness. Analogs display similarity in terms of difference.

Homologs display difference in terms of similarity. Replicas display sameness in terms of similarity. Varieties display similarity in terms of sameness.

*

Representation and Contrast

These nine modes of representation and contrast constitute the logic of representation and contrast, of comparative perceptual differentiation, of the nesting complexity of perceptions vis-a-vis one another as parts and wholes that are the same, similar, and different. Anything we can differentiate in terms of the logic of representation and contrast qualifies as a perception.

The differential representational logic of perceptions is not a predicate logic, or a sentential logic, or any other sort of logic of language. Nor is it a symbolic or uninterpreted logic, or any sort of pure logic or meta-logic or mathematical logic. Nor is it a logic of physics, or psychology, or any sort of science. Nor is it any sort of non-logic or anti-logic. The logic of perceptions is the logic of representation and contrast.

The logic of representation and contrast is not a condition of consciousness, for we are conscious of more than we are able to differentiate as perceptions. It is merely a condition of perception. Our consciousness of non-perceptions—the soul and its various modifications, including will and emotion—lacks the representational difference, the discursive display, characteristic of perceptions.

The soul and its modifications have no complexity. The soul and its modifications have the quality not of unfolding complexity but of undifferentiated impact (will and emotion). Souls display no parts or wholes. They cannot be represented.

*

The four modes at the corners of the diagram above—identities, pictures, functions, and contingencies—are the simplest combinations of representation and contrast. They are the possibilities that remain in a world with no similarity, with all perceptions either the same or different from one another, say black or white, on or off, hot or cold, 0 or 1, etc.

In such a simple, two-dimensional, digitalized world, identities, pictures, functions, and contingencies would be the only way perceptions could stand vis-a-vis one another. They would constitute an exhaustive representational logic for that world.

Let us first consider this simpler world of identities, pictures, functions, and contingencies, and then go on to consider the more complex representational modes involving similarity.

*

1) Identities

Perceptions are identical to one another if they use the same parts to display the same forms.

If the parts of one perception combine so as to display the same forms displayed by another perception, and if each of these parts in turn displays forms which are the same as those displayed by corresponding parts in the other perception, and so on for the parts of those parts as far as we can distinguish, without remainder, then the perceptions will be (for us) identical.

The forms displayed by identical perceptions include the forms of their parts, and the forms of the parts of their parts, and so on. All the parts of perceptions identical to one another—the parts of their parts, the parts of the parts of their parts, and so on—combine without remainder to display the same forms throughout.

Perceptions identical to one another everywhere display the same forms. This does not mean that they are uniform, that the forms displayed by their parts must be the same as those displayed by their wholes, although this may be so. When the parts and wholes are the same we have uniformity, as in two identical paint samples, or in a patch of fog. When they differ we have internally differentiated objects, like two coins, which, however, are still identical to one another.

We cannot fail to notice that perceptions are identical insofar as we see that without exception they display the same forms using the same parts. Suppose I have before me two coins, say two United States quarters, each with the same figures, dates, and other markings stamped on each side. These coins are identical. There is no discernible difference between them. This mean I cannot not tell from the coins themselves any difference between them.

When I recognize them, lying side by side before me, as identical with one another, I do so not because they are side by side, or because in any situation I can substitute either of them for the other, or for any other reason. I recognize them as identical simply because each displays to me the same forms using the same parts. Each coin testifies to its identity with the other.

That I am in a position to compare their testimony when they are side by side before me establishes their identity for me, not for them. In the absence of counter-evidence, I presume the coins to continue to be identical, once I have recognized them as such, whether or not I continue to compare them.

I can recognize coins in simultaneous identity with one another without question. But what about perceptions standing in successive identity? If I leave a book lying on a table and return later to find it, I recognize the book I find to be the book I left only by relying on the presumption (in the absence of contrary evidence) of their identity, that is, by presuming that when I return I find the same forms displayed by the same parts as when I left.

But since I cannot establish any direct comparison with the original book—since I can no longer bring it and the book I see now into the terms of a perception whose parts are simultaneously before me as an object—how can I know if the books are identical? To be sure, I have a mental image representing the original book. But my mental image is not the original book. It is a thought, a perception, that is identical neither to the original book nor to the book I encounter upon my return. No thought can be presumed to be identical to the original book.

It is often assumed that identity depends upon the recognition of a relationship between the object at hand (the book I now encounter) and another object (the original book). The assumption is that I must somehow be able to relate the former to the latter to establish their identity.

But relating perceptions with one another is not a criterion of their identity (or non-identity), just as relating representations of any sort is not a criterion of their being representations. I do not recognize perceptions as identical to one another because I can relate them together.

Recognizing the book I find on the table to be identical to the one I left there does not depend on somehow matching one perception with another (even if I can do so). An inability to establish a basis for comparison does not preclude identity. It precludes only the basis for comparison that would make an identity, if there is one, evident to me.

Since identity among perceptions is not a function of how they are related to one another, I do not need to reject identity because I cannot relate (and compare) perceptions whose identity is in question. In the absence of opposing testimony, I can only presume identity among such perceptions. When I find the book on the table to be identical to the one I left there, I am presuming it is so based on the unchallenged testimony of the book itself.

I can only presume (in the absence of anything to indicate otherwise) that for any perception available to me there are further perceptions, whether available to me or not, that are identical to it. I must rely on the book I find on the table being identical to the one I left there—in the absence of counter-evidence—or else I would never be able to get on with picking up the book and going about my life. My world would fall apart. I would become an amnesiac, recognizing little.

What occurs is that the book *recognizes itself to me* as the book I left on the table. The book is its own reminder of itself, its own memory. There is no organ of memory, in my brain or anywhere else. The representational capacity of perceptions is memory itself.

I cannot say how it is that a perception I encounter now is identical to one I encountered earlier. I cannot say how a perception successively displays itself to me. I can only see that it does so if it does so. To ask how this is so presumes some extraneous criterion of identity, whereas identity constitutes its own criterion. There is no way to ground identity in anything other than itself.

Every perception, by virtue of offering itself in self-testimony, automatically represents every other perception identical to it, thereby representing all past and future perceptions identical to it. In this sense, I experience the past, and the present, and the future, all at once.

If I encounter the standard meter bar in Paris—presuming, as always, in the absence of evidence to the contrary, that it has remained identical with itself ever since it was made—its past (and future) appearances are automatically represented to me, even though I had never before encountered it. To see the meter bar now is to see exactly what I would have seen had I seen it, say, a hundred years ago, or, if its persists undisturbed, a hundred years from now.

To see it now is also to see it as it would be if it were destroyed and then reconstituted. To see the meter bar now is literally to see it always. In a case like this, all the past and future instances of the perception now before me are also before me.

I presume all perceptions to stand as memories of themselves, except insofar as I have contrary testimony. Contrary testimony can only be the primitive recognition of a difference. I look at my face in the mirror every morning and it usually manages a reassuring re-display of itself. But sometimes there is a difference: a wrinkle, a grey hair, a blemish.

Such a contrast among perceptions is no more a matter of the relations among the perceptions contrasted than is representation a matter of the relations among the perceptions represented. We presume the primitive recognition of contrast among successive perceptions in the absence of contrary evidence, just as we presume the primitive recognition of representation in the absence of contrary evidence.

Representation and contrast are each negated only by the other. Neither, being primitive, can be derived from the other. And neither, by the same token, can be more fundamental than the other.

We can see how it is that everyone is sometimes mistaken about perceptions presumed to be identical to (or in contrast to) one another. I can be mistaken about the book I left on the table if someone substitutes another copy of the book for the original and I fail to notice the difference. I can mistakenly presume the book I find to be identical to the one I left—a mistaken presumption that can be sustained only by my failure to notice testimony indicating otherwise.

It is only when the book in hand is brought into comparison with a relevant perception testifying to a difference that I can discover my error. Then I have a reason to doubt that this book (the one in my hand) is the same as my book (the one I left here).

Error is never a matter of perception as such, but of some presumed comparison of perceptions.

2) Contingencies

Contingent perceptions display different forms using different parts.

Contingent perceptions are the opposite of identical perceptions. Identical perceptions are all sameness. Contingent perceptions are all difference.

If we presume the sight of milk and the smell of a rose to be contingent to one another, it is because they display without remainder different forms using different parts. Nothing about seeing milk suggests smelling a rose, and nothing about smelling a rose suggests seeing milk.

No forms at all are displayed in common by contingent perceptions. Neither the perceptions as wholes, nor the parts of the perceptions, nor the parts of their parts, and so on as far as we can distinguish, anywhere display the same (or similar) forms. All the parts of perceptions contingent to one another combine without remainder to display contrasting forms.

Since contingent perceptions in no way represent one another, they have no intrinsic capacity to remind us of one another. Only their repeated association, like thunder and lightening, can serve to allow either to remind us of the other.

Representation and Contrast

Such an association is possible, however, only in a larger perception in which the contingent perceptions are parts, for instance, the audio-visual perception of a thunderstorm. This larger perception, like any other perception, is identical with all the instances of itself, and can otherwise be represented. Its contingent parts, however, like thunder and lightening, or black and white, or sound and silence, remain perceptions contingent to one another.

As with a presumed identity, I can be in error in presuming perceptions to be contingent when actual comparison may show otherwise.

3) Pictures

Pictures display the same forms using different parts. A photograph of a friend is not composed of the same parts as is the friend himself. The one is made up of paper and photosensitive chemicals, the other of flesh and blood.

Yet the photographic print displays (at least from one perspective) the same forms as my friend exhibits in real life. We see the photograph as a picture of my friend insofar as it displays forms we also see displayed by him in real life, at least sometimes, even though the means of display (the parts) used in one case contrast with those used in the other.

Since perceptions which picture one another use different parts to display the same forms, each part of a picturing perception contrasts with its corresponding part in the perception it pictures.

I see the flesh of my friend's face on the one hand, and the coated, multi-colored, paper photographic print of his face on the other. I see them as two collections of contrasting parts even as I see that they display the same forms.

Any part of a perception which helps picture another perception displays forms which contrast with those displayed by its corresponding part in the perception it pictures.

Since perceptions which picture one another have contrasting parts, the forms of those parts do not belong to the common display.

Identities and contingencies display a consistency of parts and wholes. They are either all the same, or all different, without remainder.

Pictures, however, are representationally mixed modes. They simultaneously and obviously represent and contrast with one another. Like identities but unlike contrasts, pictures, by virtue of their representational aspect, can directly remind us of one another. But no such reminder can be mistaken for an identity. The non-picturing difference immediately testifies otherwise.

I cannot be mistaken that a photograph of a face is a picture of my friend if it is a picture of my friend, that is, if it re-displays, in part, the same forms my friend sometimes displays. In fact, it can succeed as a picture of my friend even if it was taken not of him but of someone else, say, of his identical twin brother. I might be mistaken about who was actually photographed—that is, which person—but correct that so-and-so is nonetheless represented even if he was not actually photographed.

If I am mistaken about what a photograph represents, it can only be because I fail to carry out an actual comparison between the photograph and the object or person purportedly photographed.

I might believe that a photograph of an old man is a photograph of the last surviving Civil War veteran, but I might easily be mistaken in this belief. The last Civil War veteran is dead and unavailable for comparative purposes. I cannot rely on my memory or any other evidence of the man, for I might have been deceived in some way, even if the memory-image or other evidence I now hold does indeed picture the man in the photograph.

I can be as mistaken about pictures as about identities, or any of the modes of representation and contrast. But, as with any of them, such a mistake can be revealed as a mistake only through some further comparison which provides counter-evidence. Otherwise, we not only can but do presume the veracity of the purported representation (or contrast).

4) Functions

Functions are perceptions which display contrasting forms using the same parts.

A series of contrasting structures built out of a uniform set of children's blocks will display different forms even though they are built with the same units. We can see both that those structures contrast with one another and that they are built out of the same parts.

We can see, for example, that 01 and 10 are strongly contrasting combinations of the same two numerals, 0 and 1. Since perceptions which are functions of one another use the same parts to display contrasting forms, each part of a functional perception will display the same forms as some part in the perception of which it is a function. Thus I see that the numeral 0 appears as a part in both 10 and 01 even though I also see that 10 is not 01.

Functional perceptions use the same parts to display contrasting forms. We can see not only that they display contrasting forms, but that the parts displaying those contrasting forms in each respective functional perception are the same. Since perceptions which are functions of one another have the same parts, the contrasting forms they display do not include the forms of the parts displaying those contrasting forms.

Functions, like pictures, are mixed modes. They simultaneously and obviously represent and contrast with one another. Like identities and pictures, but unlike contrasts, functions, by virtue of their representational aspect, can directly remind us of one another. But no such reminder can be mistaken for an identity. The non-functional difference immediately testifies otherwise. Functions too are subject to error arising from merely presumed comparisons.

Perceptions can be either directly or indirectly functions of one another. Perceptions that are directly functions of one another are composed of the same parts. Perceptions that are indirectly functions of one another are composed of the same parts as are found in some third perception. For instance, 97 and 79 are directly functions of one another for each is composed of exactly the same parts, namely, 7 and 9. But 397 and 542 are functions of one another only indirectly with regard to the collection of ordinary numerals: 0 1 2 3 4 5 6 7 8 9.

The parts of directly functional perceptions are the same in one perception as in another, and the parts of indirectly functional perceptions are the same as those of further perceptions of which they are both functions.

The parts of perceptions which are functions of one another may all be the same, or they may be different. Thus all models built out of matchsticks not only have the same parts as all other such models, but those parts are all the same, namely, matchsticks. On the other hand, a perception may be composed of different parts all in contrast to one another, like a kaleidoscope, and still be a function of another perception composed in a different fashion of that same variety of parts, like that same kaleidoscope shaken and reconfigured. This can occur whether or not the perceptions are directly or indirectly functions of one another.

*

Identities, contingencies, pictures, and functions exhaust the perceptual combinations in which the same forms are displayed by different parts, and different forms are displayed by the same parts.

We have seen that perceptions also display forms in which what is the same and what is different cannot clearly be separated. Perceptions which display such forms are **similar** to one another. Similar forms are neither the same nor different. They are an irreducible mixture of the two.

Similarity blends sameness and difference so seamlessly that we cannot see where one begins and the other ends. Similarity does not have the edge, the sharp boundary condition that marks both sameness and difference. Sameness and difference are neither repeated nor denied in similarity, but somehow mutually modulated.

Representation and Contrast

Similarity, which runs the full spectrum between sameness and difference, introduces uncertainty. Perceptions similar to one another are ambiguous. Similarity allows indeterminate degrees of sameness and difference.

The similarity of a maple tree and an oak tree is manifest not by the same or different forms displayed (or not displayed) by each, but by the forms each tree displays vis-a-vis the other which are neither the same nor different, but somehow both at once, or similar.

Consider a rose and a dandelion. They are neither identical or contingent. Nor are they pictures or functions. They do not use the same parts to display different forms. Nor do they use different parts to display the same forms. There is nothing about similarity that allows us to say exactly what in these perceptions is the same and what is different. We cannot isolate in any rose or dandelion, with regard to the other, specific different parts displaying the same forms, nor specific parts that are the same displaying different forms, as we can do with pictures and functions.

Similar perceptions, far from neatly parcelling out sameness and difference according to their parts and wholes, blur them together. Similarities are indeterminate; they are indistinct and uncertain. When we see similarity among perceptions we see a sameness and difference we cannot separate.

It would be reductionist to reduce similarity to terms of sameness and difference. Similarity itself is as irreducible and primitive as sameness and difference. Just as perceptions display the same forms if they display the same forms, and different forms if they display different forms, so they also display similar forms if they display similar forms. Perceptions displaying similar wholes, parts, or both are kinds, analogues, homologues, replicas, and varieties. And just as we can be in error over presumed comparisons of sameness and difference, so we can err over presumed comparisons involving similarities.

The remaining modes of representation and contrast exhibit varying degrees of similarity.

*

5) Kinds

Perceptions are kinds of one another insofar as they display similar forms using similar parts. If we recognize two cows, or two trees, or two mountains, or two cities, as kinds of one another it is because the items in each pair display similar forms using similar parts.

If I recognize two trees to be kinds of one another, it is because I recognize similar forms such as leaves, branches, trunks, and roots in each displaying similar parts such as blades, veins, and photosynthetic cells, etc. As the examples suggest, species are kinds. The similar forms displayed by perceptions that are kinds include the forms of their parts, and the forms of the parts of their parts, and so on as far as we can distinguish without remainder. Kinds, like identities and contingencies, are consistent in their display of parts and wholes.

6) Analogues

Analogues are perceptions which display similar forms using different parts. They, along with the homologues, replicas, and varieties to be discussed below, are mixed modes of representation, like pictures and functions.

If we recognize umbrellas and penises, computers and brains, beehives and cities, and eyes and cameras as analogous pairs, it is because they display similar forms using different parts. Eyes are made of flesh and blood and cameras of plastic, metal, and glass. Yet their respective parts are so combined in each as to produce perceptions which display similar forms. Both are enclosed chambers into which light enters through a small opening, passes through a lens, and projects an image on a screen.

If eyes and cameras displayed the same forms using different parts, they would picture one another. A camera might be designed that looked just like an eye, or a living creature might be found somewhere whose eyes looked just like some camera.

7) Homologues

Perceptions are homologues of one another insofar as they display different forms using similar parts. We recognize the sexual organs of men and women, or two Mondrian paintings, or Chinese checkers and conventional checkers, or grated garlic and chopped onions, as pairs that are respectively homologues to each another because they display different forms using similar parts.

The sexual organs of men and women display different forms using similar parts. The similar parts are tissues and the different forms are the gross contrasting arrangements these tissues display: penises and clitorises, etc.

We can see that homologous perceptions use similar parts to display contrasting forms since we can see not only that they display forms which contrast with one another, but also that the parts that display these contrasting forms in each homologous perception are themselves similar to one another. Perceptions can be either directly or indirectly homologs of one another, just as perceptions can be either directly or indirectly functions of one another.

8) Replicas

Perceptions are replicas of one another insofar as they display the same forms using similar parts. A counterfeit twenty-dollar bill and a legitimate twenty-dollar bill, a forgery of an Old Master and that Old Master itself, a typescript page and a photocopy of that typescript—all these are replicas of one another.

A genuine twenty-dollar bill and a counterfeit are copies insofar as they display the same forms using similar parts. Certain details of the engraving, the textures, etc., of the bills will be similar rather than the same. If those details were the same rather than similar, the two bills would be identical to rather than replicas of one another. Both bills in that case would be genuine, that is, "perfect" counterfeits. If their details were different rather than similar, the two bills would be pictures rather than replicas of one another (the parts of each would stand in contrast to those of the other).

Since perceptions which are replicas of one another have similar parts, the forms displayed by such perceptions include more or less the forms of their parts, and more or less the forms of the parts of those parts, and so on. The parts of perceptions which are replicas of one another themselves display forms whose similarity allows them to be more or less included in the forms of the perceptions which are replicas of one another.

9) Varieties

Perceptions are varieties of one another insofar as they display similar forms using the same parts. If we recognize a road map of North Dakota and one of West Virginia, a king's pawn chess opening and a queen's pawn opening, and a mirror image of myself and a mirror image of my mirror image, as varieties of one another, it is because they display similar forms using the same parts.

The same brand-name road maps of North Dakota and West Virginia use the same parts to display similar forms. These parts include the layout of that brand—the type-settings for place-names, the numerals and symbols of highway numbers, the graphic icons for roads and highways, as well as for cities, natural features, political boundaries, and other items. The similar forms include the overall patterns displayed by these parts in each map.

If the forms displayed by their parts were the same rather than similar, the two maps would be identical rather than varieties of one another. If those forms were different rather than similar, the two maps would be functions rather than varieties of one another. Varieties—like functions and homologs—can be either directly or indirectly varieties of one another.

Just as we can see that to be similar is not to be the same, so we can see that to be similar is not to be different. Identical maps are identical to the extent to which they are the same, and functional maps are functions to the extent to which they are partly the same and partly different. Maps that are varieties are varieties to the extent to which they are partly the same and partly similar. We are familiar with maps that are identical and maps that are varieties. But maps that are

Representation and Contrast 37

functions of one another are just as common. Maps that are functions of one another use the same markings, shapes, symbols, etc., to display forms that are different.

In the case of my mirror image and a subsequent mirror image of my mirror image, the parts are the same. These include the visual components of line, color, shape, and so on. But the forms displayed by those parts are similar rather than the same. The similarity lies in the reversal of the overall patterns displayed. The first mirror image of my face and the mirror image of that image stand in overall left-right inversion. They display forms that are similar (if peculiarly so) using parts that are the same (any point in a mirror is the same as its mirror-image).

*

There are some perceptions which actually display the modes of representation and contrast. We can have a perception whose parts are all identical to one another; a perception whose parts are all replicas of one another; a perception whose parts are all pictures of one another; and so on for each of the modes of representation and contrast.

Insofar as the parts of a perception are all identical to one another, that perception is a **field**, a uniform, homogeneous spread, such as a homogeneous surface, or color, or tone, or a volume. Fields are as diverse as a patch of fog, a sustained high C, or a bar of pure gold.

Insofar as the parts of a perception are contingent to one another, that perception is **chaos**. A jumble of different parts, representationally opaque to one another, vertiginous and dissonant, is chaos, as in any mess (explosions, rubble, litter, confusion, static, etc.).

Of the intermediate modes of representation displayed in specific perceptions, perhaps the most familiar is the **group** constituted out of kinds—a species or genus whose parts are all themselves kinds of one another, as in herd of holstein cows, or a flock of blackbirds, or several strata of limestone rock, or a cluster of galaxies.

Insofar as the parts of a perception are functions of one another, that perception is a **system**. Common notations such as an alphabetic script or a numerical calculation, for instance, Arabic numerals, or Mayan bars and dots, or Roman letters, are systems. Some natural systems include the genetic code and the chemical table of the elements.

Insofar as the parts of a perception are pictures of one another, that perception is a **theme**, a collection of the same image differently displayed. An exhibition of different photographs of a single subject, say Abraham Lincoln, constitutes a theme. The spherical nature of otherwise different heavenly bodies (suns, planets, and moons) makes for another theme.

Insofar as the parts of a perception are analogues of one another, that perception is a **type**. For example, a collection of public ways, such as paths, roads, highways, railways, canals, etc., is a type. A type is marked by the similarity displayed by its mutually analogous parts.

Insofar as the parts of a perception are homologues of one another, that perception is a **mosaic**. For example, a decorative pattern using similar items differently arranged is a mosaic. A mosaic is a collection of homologues, or differences whose parts are similar rather than the same, as they are in a system.

Insofar as the parts of a perception are varieties of one another, that perception is a **genre**. For example, the use of the same parts (the words of English speech) to elaborate similar forms (such as those of prose as opposed to verse) is a genre. By genre I mean a collection of varieties, or similarities, whose parts are the same.

And, finally, insofar as the parts of a perception are replicas of one another, that perception is an **spectrum**. For example, a standard color sampler from a paint store is a spectrum. A spectrum is marked by the sameness displayed by its mutually picturing parts.

*

There are further aspects of perceptions, apart from sameness, similarity, and difference, by which they can be distinguished. These are the specific qualities of perceptions. Any non-representational aspect of any perception is a specific quality of that perception.

Perceptions are variously beautiful, unjust, melancholy, lovable, expensive, tiresome, durable, useful, frustrating, fearsome, desirable, and so on. Such qualities concern the specific forms perceptions exhibit as parts and as wholes. Unlike the representational qualities of sameness, similarity, and difference, which hold regardless of the specific forms that perceptions display, the non-representational values of perceptions depend upon the specific nature of the forms displayed.

Although all perceptions are the same, similar, or different vis-a-vis one another, not all perceptions are beautiful, just, and so on, vis-a-vis one another. Beauty, justice, and other such comparisons among perceptions depend on the actual such-and-such of the perceptions compared, on their specific qualities.

Justice is a certain comparative display of perceptions, as is beauty, generosity, and every other value. To know justice is to see just acts, to know beauty is to see beautiful things, and so on. Even values depending on the partness of a perception, like use, depend upon the larger whole that that perception helps display.

We cannot generically represent justice, beauty, or any other specific comparison, any more than we can generically represent identity, picturing, and the other modes of representation. We can only represent perceptions that are just, beautiful, etc. To treat any specific quality displayed by some perceptions, such as justice or beauty, as if it were a general quality characteristic of all perception is to judge all perceptions erroneously by the criterion of certain specific perceptions.

Since all perceptions are not the same or similar in this way, we can persist in asserting they are only at the cost of distorting the world of perceptions. We need not deny justice, beauty, or any other specific configuration of forms to acknowledge that they need not be characteristic of all perceptions.

Neither can we treat such qualities as mere relations among perceptions. Relations are always displayed by perceptions, and never revealed independently of them. To maintain that specific qualities are nothing more than relations is to deny that they can be represented at all, for only perceptions can be represented, and, as we have seen, we cannot represent any relation, only some perception in which it is displayed.

*

Some general comments:

The logic of representation and contrast—of nesting parts and wholes—overcomes the Parmenidean split of perception into form and content, order and chaos, permanence and change, one and many, etc.

Form is not separate from content; the two are not somehow distinct things that have to be synthesized, but simply one thing—a perception—that we can 'see' in two different ways.

Any perception is simultaneously form and content, order and chaos, permanence and change, a one and a many, etc. It is a form with regard to its own parts, and a part with regard to some other form. Any perception is at once orderly and chaotic, permanent and changing, object and event, a one and a many.

Formal order is displayed in chaotic perception, like a steady but pulsating image on the television screen, or the retina. Formal order endures through perception, exuding permanence in its sustained oneness; but it also remains subject to change, to taking its place among the many: the picture on the television screen, or the retina, can change at any moment.

Successive identities are the most enduring objects; successive contingencies are the most abrupt events. The other modes of representation and contrast—varieties, replicas, pictures, kinds, functions, homologs, and analogs—constitute a kind of wavy spectrum between identities and contingencies.

The logic of representation and contrast tells us nothing about any specific object and/or event, any specific perception. It only tells us the possible ways in which any perception must stand vis-a-vis other perceptions. Unlike traditional formal systems, it takes itself as its own 'interpretation,' as it own content, thereby ceasing to be 'form' distinct from content. The logic of representation and contrast does not describe a system of forms. Its key terms—"sameness," "similarity," and "difference"—only point us towards the comparisons implicit in the very act of distinguishing perceptions from one another.

There can be no representation (or contrast) of the logic of representation and contrast. There can be no representation (or contrast) of identity, kindness, contingency, and the rest. All that can be represented (or contrasted) are perceptions that are identical, perceptions that are kinds, and so on. No representation (or contrast) can itself ever be represented (or contrasted).

Neither is the logic of representation and contrast a question of relations among the perceptions that represent or contrast with one another. Whether or not perceptions stand related has nothing to do with whether or not they represent or contrast with one another.

Identity, kindness, and all the other modes of representation and contrast arise given the display of forms by perceptions. They cannot be characterized other than to say that they do so arise: that perceptions display forms, that those forms are the same, similar, or different, and so on. We can say that perceptions that are the same have perceptions as parts that are the same, etc., and so on for perceptions that are similar and different, but sameness, similarity, and difference themselves remain as ineffable as they are obvious.

There can be no explanation which somehow answers questions such as: What is identity? What is kindness? What is contingency? What is representation? What is contrast? What is sameness? What is difference? Rather, the only possible answers are mute ones—dumb gestures—such as this text—pointing to the obvious.

What cannot be perceived, what does not fulfill the logic of representation and contrast—e.g., the soul—is neither one nor many, order nor chaos, permanent nor changing. It lacks the differentiating part and whole complexity of perception. It is neither identical with other non-perceptions, nor contingent to them, nor a kind to them, nor does it stand to them in any other representational mode.

CHAPTER THREE

Sensations and Thoughts

Perceptions are inherently representational. They exhibit the differential logic of representation and contrast.

The perceptions of which we are conscious are also specific perceptions displaying specific forms. In this chapter we will consider the major specific perceptions of our experience: sensations and thoughts. Examining sensations and thoughts in terms of the logic of representation and contrast will further our understanding of perception.

Even though any specific perception must stand vis-a-vis other perceptions as an identity, a contingency, and so on as the case may be, the specific forms displayed by that perception are what give it the specific character or quality that it has.

There are an indefinite number of specific forms displayed by perceptions, but all of them are either sensations or thoughts, that is, all perceptions—at least for us—are either sensation-perceptions or thought-perceptions.

There are five distinct sensation-perceptions and one distinct thought-perception. The five sensation-perceptions correspond to the five senses. These are the perceptions we see, touch, hear, taste, and smell. The thought-perceptions correspond to what we remember and what we imagine. Our thoughts are mental images.

Some sensations include: seeing my hand; feeling the texture and resistance of a doorknob; hearing a musical tone; tasting a grain of salt; smelling a rose. Some thoughts include: recalling my mother's face; imagining a trip to Mexico; entertaining a fantasy about life in Atlantis; constructing a thought-experiment involving frictionless surfaces.

Our thoughts, it cannot be overemphasized, are not to be confused with concepts, those spurious abstractions from sensations. Thoughts are not independent, pure abstractions existing in something called a mind—Aristotle's 'place of forms.' Thoughts are concrete images, actual perceptions; and what I call 'mind' is in fact what is meant by memory and imagination, and not at all the traditional conceptual notion of mind.

Our sensation-perceptions and thought-perceptions vary immensely in grossness and subtlety.

Sensation-perceptions, unlike thought-perceptions, come to us through our bodies. Of our sensation-perceptions, our tactile-perceptions are the grossest. They manifest the impact and resistance of matter and force. The quality of tactile impact is pressure, which may be pleasurable or painful.

Our gustatory-perceptions are less gross. They manifest, via the measure of our tongues, not the pressure of tactile impact but a wholly different spectrum of taste: the spectrum of sweet, sour, bitter, and salty.

Our olfactory-perceptions are still less gross. They manifest, via the measure of our noses, yet another, even more subtle sense, this one revealing the richer spectrum of smell.

Even more subtle are our audible-perceptions. They manifest, vis the measure of our ears, the complex spectrum of sound.

But the most subtle of our sensations are our visual-perceptions. They manifest, via the measure of our eyes, the visual spectrum. The very great subtlety of light is demonstrated by its marginal material-

Sensations and Thoughts

ity. Although our physical bodies are sensitive to light, light itself has zero at-rest inertia. All of its mass has been transformed into energy.

Finally, our thought-perceptions are the most subtle of all. They are, as we shall see, entirely beyond the physical realm of mass and energy.

*

Each of the five sensation-perceptions has as its parts only those sensations which belong to that specific sensation. Thus touches or tactions are composed only of tactions; tastes are composed only of tastes; smells are composed only of smells; sounds are composed only of sounds; and sights are composed only of sights. Thoughts too have only thoughts as parts.

It would be absurd for a sound to be part of a sight, or a taste to be part of a smell, or a sound to be part of a thought. This means, in terms of the logic of representation and contrast, that touches, tastes, smells, sounds, sights, and thoughts all stand in contrast to one another, even though they can be combined together in various ways to constitute larger, more inclusive perceptions.

Our sensations are composed either of tactions, or tastes, or smells, or sounds, or sights, or various combinations of these. Since tactions, tastes, smells, sounds, and sights all stand in contrast to one another, combinations of two or more of these constitute perceptions whose parts stand in contrast to one another.

Perceptions constituted through combinations of different sensations include the ordinary objects we encounter: sticks and stones, earth and air, fire and water, tables and chairs, and so on. A stone or a table is not simply something we see. It is also something we touch (if we feel it), or hear (if we tap it), or taste (if we put our tongues to it), or smell (if we put our noses to it).

Each of the different sensation perceptions, when combined, displays forms which may be the same, similar, or different vis-a-vis one another. A perception we see may display the same forms (using different parts) as a perception we touch. Or it may display similar or different forms. Where the same forms are displayed, the visual parts picture the tactile parts; where similar forms are displayed, the visual parts are analogous to the tactile parts; where different forms are displayed, the visual parts are contingent to the tactile parts.

Ordinary physical objects and events consistently picture one another through the different senses. What we call ordinary objects are perceptual pictures. They display the same forms using different parts (visual, tactile, etc.). Perceptions whose parts stand as analogs or contingencies to one another—analogs and types—are not ordinary objects or events at all.

*

Consider an ordinary object like a stone. Its visual parts consistently stand in one-to-one correspondence with its tactile parts, so that each group of parts (the visual and the tactile) displays the same forms, even though the parts of one group differ from those of the other (visual perceptions not being tactile perceptions).

We do not frequently encounter stones as sounds, tastes, or smells. Normally there is not evident any audible stone which pictures both the tactile stone and the visual stone. Nor are there normally evident any corresponding gustatory or olfactory stones. But if I tap the surface of the visual/tactile stone, certain pitches emitted will correspond to certain visual and tactile parts (that is, certain colors and contacts). And I can produce in this manner an audible stone which indeed pictures the visual and tactile stones already familiar to me. Similarly, I can taste the stone, smell the stone, etc. Representationally, an ordinary object is not an inert mass of some kind of stuff. It is a picture: a specific *display* reproduced in different modes (sights, sounds, etc.).

The idea that our sensations are composed of contrasting groups of parts was developed by the great philosopher George Berkeley. In *A Treatise Concerning the Principles of Human Knowledge*, section 1, he writes:

"By sight I have the ideas of light and colors, with their several degrees and variations. By touch I perceive, for example, hard and soft, heat and cold, motion and resistance, and of all these more and less either as to quantity or degree. Smelling furnishes me with odors, the palate with tastes, and hearing conveys sounds to the mind in all their variety of tone and composition. And as several of these are observed to accompany each other, they come to be marked by one name, and so to be reputed as one thing. Thus, for example, a certain color, taste, smell, figure, and consistence having been observed to go together are accounted one distinct thing signified by the name 'apple'; other collections of ideas constitute a stone, a tree, a book, and the like sensible things—which as they are pleasing or disagreeable excite the passions of love, hatred, joy, grief, and so forth."

Berkeley is famous for his denial of material substance. He argued that our sensations are not representations of anything 'out there,' but the irreducible raw material of our experience. The conventional interpretation of his work is that, having denied material substance, he made sensations the attributes of mental substance. All sensations, as he put it, exist in some mind, either ours or God's.

One may accept Berkeley's denial of material substance without concluding that sensations belong in the mind. Indeed, I propose that the contents of mind—our thoughts—are perceptions as irreducible as our sensations, and quite distinct from them. Far from constituting any mental substance, our thoughts, like our sensations, are perceptions subject to the logic of representation and contrast. We are not minds conscious of sensations, as Berkeley would have it, but souls conscious of perceptions which are both thoughts and sensations.

*

Just as sensations can only be sensed (that is, seen, heard, etc.), and not thought, so thoughts can only be thought, not sensed. It can be seen that a ball is thrown for a dog, and it can be imagined that a ball is thrown for a dog, but imagining it is not seeing it (it is imagining it); and seeing it is not imagining it (it is seeing it).

Even though it can be seen that sights are seen, and even though it can be thought that thoughts are thought, it cannot be seen that thoughts are thought, and it cannot be thought that sights are seen. In the same way, it cannot be seen that something is heard, nor felt that something is smelt, nor heard that something is seen, and so on. Each sense has its own integrity; it is different from the others. Thoughts too have their own integrity. Thoughts are like a sixth sense.

Consider the integrity of different perceptions, for example, a visible perception and an audible perception. The sight of a tap-dancer's feet tap-dancing is a visible perception; the sound of his tap-dancing is an audible perception. These perceptions are different and yet they picture one another. They both display the same forms using different parts. The forms we *see* displayed in one case we *hear* displayed in the other, although we can no more see the forms we hear displayed than we can hear the forms we see displayed. Only by seeing each dancing step *while* hearing each corresponding dancing tap do we establish a correspondence between seeing and hearing.

Once a correlation between the tap-dancer's visual feet and the audible music of his tapping is established, we are in a position to appreciate whether or not they display forms that represent or contrast with one another, for we cannot see or hear separately that they do so. We do not merely hear or merely see the tap dancing; rather we see-hear it. In turns out, in this case, that they picture one another. The same process of correlation and comparison goes as well for the rest of our senses, and for our thoughts.

Even though tactions, tastes, smells, sounds, sights, and thoughts each stand in contrast to the others, it does not follow that the perceptions they each display are all the same or similar with regard to one another. All thoughts are not similar or identical to all other thoughts, nor all sights to all other sights, and so on for the other sensations.

Even though thoughts, tactions, tastes, smells, sounds, and sights, each stand in contrast to the others, each can also stand in contrast to itself. Indeed, thoughts that are the same, similar, or different vis-a-vis one another can thereby stand with regard to one another in any aspect of representation and contrast. And so too for sights, sounds, tactions, tastes, and smells.

On the other hand, since, for instance, sights stand in contrast to non-sights, sights can stand with regard to non-sights *only* as pictures, analogs or contingencies, and *never* as identities, kinds, functions, replicas, homologs, or varieties; and so too for thoughts, sounds, and the rest.

A thought can never be identical to a sight, a sound, or any non-thought. Neither can a thought be a kind, a homolog, a function, a replica, or a variety of a non-thought. And so too with sights and non-sights, sounds and non-sounds, and the rest.

In sum, thoughts and the five sensations each can stand to the others *only* as pictures, analogs, and contingencies since their respective parts (thoughts, sights, sounds, etc.) stand in contrast to one another. Yet thoughts can stand with respect to other thoughts not only as pictures, analogs, and contingencies, but also as identities, replicas, kinds, varieties, functions, and homologs; and so too can sights stand with regard to other sights in the full range of representation and contrast; and so too can sounds with regard to other sounds; and so on for the other senses.

*

It follows that thoughts and the five senses *cannot* be defined in terms of the logic of representation and contrast.

We cannot distinguish perceptions as thoughts, sounds, etc., merely on the basis of the representational logic they share as perceptions.

Thoughts, sights, sounds, etc., are distinguished from one another not by the logic of representation and contrast but by certain specific perceptions which stand as the condition of our having the thoughts we have, the sights we have, and so on.

For instance, I see sights, and among the sights I see is the specific sight of my body, which more or less accompanies all my sights. I can usually see my body, or parts of it, when I am generally about seeing whatever it is that I see. More specifically, I can see (perhaps using mirrors and other instruments) that it is my eyes and related tissues (optic nerves, etc.) which accompany the sights that I see. Moreover, I also see that there are other bodies more or less like my own, with eyes, optic nerves, and so on, also more or less like my own.

When I see my eyes and other eyes I see certain sights among many sights. I do not see sights being seen. To see that I have eyes and a body is not to see that I see. To see that others have eyes and bodies is not to see that they see. But to see my own body and eyes is to see a condition of my seeing, for it seems I cannot see without a body, and specifically not without eyes, at least not in my waking consciousness. And to see that there are other bodies with eyes is to see that there are other conditions for seeing like my own (whether or not those conditions are fulfilled).

To see these conditions distributed among other bodies like my own is to see that (though not how) seeing *can* be open to others like myself. It is to see that there are public conditions of seeing. It is these conditions (themselves seen) which are the conditions by which we distinguish sights from non-sights. Sights are what we see, and we see them on the condition of having eyes, which are supported by a body we can see, etc.

My visual body (the one I see) is accompanied by a tactile body I can feel (my flesh and bone), an audible body I can hear (say, if it is percussed), an aromatic body I can smell, and a flavorful body I can taste. To feel my own body is to feel a condition of my feeling (presumably I can touch or feel nothing without my body). To hear my own body is to hear a condition of my hearing (presumably I can hear nothing without my body). And so on for smelling and tasting.

I distinguish tactions (touches or feelings) from non-tactions on the basis of certain tactions, namely, those of the flesh of my body. I feel the flesh of my body as the condition of my feeling any tactions at all, from bumping into the furniture to making love. The distribution of flesh in my body and in the bodies of others, testifies, like the distribution of eyes, to the openness or publicity of tactions.

Similarly, I distinguish sounds from non-sounds on the basis of certain sounds, namely, the various sounds of my body, including my ears. My ears are the condition of my hearing and I hear my ears when I manipulate them (scratch them, rub them, pop them, plug them, etc.). The sound of my ears is a kind of swishing, rushing sound I hear when I rub them.

Sensations and Thoughts

Although I rarely if ever hear ears other than my own, I do hear certain bodily sounds from other bodies like those I hear from my own—most obviously, voices. Voices are not a condition of hearing, but, since clear speech (the more or less accurate reproduction of an accent or dialect) depends upon hearing, the voices of others testify to the openness or publicity of hearing.

I distinguish tastes from non-tastes on the basis of certain tastes, namely, the tastes of my own body, and especially, my own mouth. The taste of my mouth is the condition of my tasting anything at all, and to taste mouths other than my own (say, in kissing) is to taste other conditions for tasting more or less like my own. So the distribution of mouths and tongues testifies to the publicity of tastes.

Finally, I distinguish smells from non-smells on the basis of certain smells, namely, various smells of my body. The smells of my body (or some of them) are the condition of my smelling anything at all, and to smell smells more or less like those, but on other bodies, is to smell other conditions for smelling more or less like my own. So the distribution of bodily smells also testifies to the publicity of smells.

My point is that each of our five senses is revealed to us as a sense only on the condition of certain accompanying privileged instances of that sense. These privileged instances are concentrated in our bodies, and particularly in our sense organs and ultimately our brains. It is the sum of these that constitutes what we take to be our bodies. In the end, for something to count as part of my body it needs to be a condition of one of my physical senses.

The fleshy body, infused with nerves, is the sense organ for touch, with the nose, tongue, ears, and eyes the sense organs for the other sensations. Different as we have seen the five senses to be for consciousness, in the body their organs are meshed together into a common nervous system culminating in the brain. The different sense organs are adapted to the different perceptions they receive and transmit to the brain. Our sense organs are like different tuners receiving different signals: audio, visual, gustatory, feeling, and olfactory. The brain, via the network of neurological cells, is the receiver of these signals.

But in the brain these impulses mysteriously disappear. Consciousness of sensations cannot be said to occur in the brain, or in any other physical location, although it seems that sensations somehow come to consciousness through the brain.

*

Thoughts constitute a sort of sixth sense.

They differ from the five physical senses in not displaying any condition of access. I have no thought-organ of thought. I cannot think any distinguishing thought of thinking the way I can see a distinguishing sight of seeing, hear a distinguishing sound of hearing, and so on for the other sensations.

If sights were like thoughts, we would be able to see without any distinguishing conditions of sight; no eyes, brains, etc., would be needed. Under such circumstances, I could never see, from anything I saw, whether or not anyone else ever saw anything. Yet this is exactly the situation in which I find myself with regard to my thoughts.

Among my thoughts there is no peculiar, self-revelatory, distinguishing thought of any condition of thought. If I am confident that others have thoughts, it is only because I presume that other bodies like mine are accompanied by thoughts such as those which accompany my body.

I can distinguish thoughts only by comparison with non-thoughts, and then only negatively. I distinguish certain perceptions as thoughts only because, unlike sensations, they display no self-conditioning.

Sight can be effected by disease or injury to the eye, and hearing can be effected by disease or injury to the ears, and so on for the other senses, but there is no direct evidence that thought can be effected by bodily injury. Of course, injury to the brain can produce senility, aphasia, and other conditions. But what is affected here is not thought itself, so far as anyone can tell, but only the ability to express thought in sensation and to recognize certain sensations as expressions of thought.

Sensations and Thoughts

This apparent loss of memory and imagination (due to physical trauma, drugs, etc.) does not mean that we need a body to have thoughts (as we need one to have sensations). Damage to sensations alone, that is, to our body-dependent ability to fully entertain sensations, is itself sufficient to effect the representational disconnection between them. An amnesiac, for all we know, might be able disconnectedly to remember his mother without being able to recognize that the woman who visits him is his mother. The possibility remains that I can think without a brain. As long as no physical connection is established between brains and thoughts, it remains possible for there to be thoughts unconditioned by brains, as well as brains unconditioned by thoughts.

Indeed, there is no evidence that thoughts are sensations, that is, brain-dependent, and considerable evidence that they are not sensations. If thoughts are not sensations, we do not necessarily need a body to think. If we could think a condition of thought, we would have to think it, not see it, or hear it, etc. We would have to think a thought that, among thoughts, would correspond to what, among sensations, we call our body. It would be an inescapable thought-body without which we could not have any thoughts at all.

But since we cannot think any such condition of thought, we cannot think how it is that we think. Thoughts are quite unlike sensations, with their bodily organs. They are mysterious in a way sensations can never be. As long as bodies can be seen, touched, etc., but not thought, they can no more give us a clue to thought than thunder can give a blind man a clue to lightning.

I conclude, given the distribution of living bodies like mine, that there are others who have thoughts, just as I conclude, given the distribution of conditioning eyes, that there are others who have sights. And since I see eyes among the sights I see, the publicity of seeing is itself something seen.

But since I do not think any condition of thinking among the thoughts I think, the publicity of thinking cannot be thought. I cannot find in thoughts the evidence for publicity that I find in sensations. I can find no thought-organ corresponding to my sense-organs. My thoughts remain private; my sensations public.

Lacking among themselves any self-conditioning point, my private thoughts maintain a detached, disembodied character. They stand unoriented to the body, free from the conditions that obtain among sensations. This leaves them wildly ungrounded compared to sensations. Even thoughts of the body have, in thought, no privilege over other thoughts.

It is in our thoughts that we are disembodied beings. It is there that we enjoy a realm of perceptions within which there is no conditioning perception, no fixed reference, no point of articulation, no center, no ground, no foundation, no criterion. Thoughts exhibit a wild, undomesticated freedom. They do not know themselves to be bound in any way.

This riot of the mind—going anywhere, anytime, in no time—is conspicuously absent in sensation. In sensation we are bound to the body. We are somewhere, at sometime, and everything takes time. The laws of physics need not hold among thoughts, but always hold among sensations. My sensations hold together with a reliable consistency conspicuously missing among my thoughts.

My movements in thought do not require a thought-body, while my movements in sensation always require a sensation-body. I can move or float through thoughts simply as a detached awareness, something I cannot do with sensations. I am bonded with my sensations through my body, but nothing similar bonds me to my thoughts.

*

The stubborn patterning of sensations (always implicit if not apparent) is the most prominent feature of their self-conditioning, just as the freedom and abandon of thought (always implicit, if not always apparent) is the most prominent feature of the non-conditioning of thoughts. It is the business of physics to mark this stubborn patterning among sensations. This amounts to tracing their consistent, external relations, their regularly recurring relations.

Sensations have a distinct scientific logic. They are often repetitively, reliably, predictable. In this sense, they are unambiguous and undissimulating. All points in spacetime are clearly and distinctly

Sensations and Thoughts 55

themselves, and not to be mistaken for any others. Even in quantum physics, where the behavior of subatomic particles and forces cannot be unambiguously anticipated, that behavior itself remains quite unambiguous, however and wherever it is isolated.

The logic of thoughts, on the other hand, is a polyvocal, either/and/or logic; it is an ambiguous, dissimulating logic. There can be no science of the mind paralleling the science of sensation for the external relations between thoughts are entirely free and unconditioned: any thought in principle can be substituted for any other, so that any relation can obtain among any thoughts.

We find the apparently unlimited free association of thoughts in our power of imagination. Virtually anything imaginable can happen in thought, and often does. Virtually any thoughts can be associated with any others, something unthinkable in sensation, where association is governed by the laws of physics.

Since any relation can obtain among thoughts, there is little point in charting relations among thoughts. What matters in thought is the configuration of forms displayed by any thought, its internal rather than its external relations. The logic of thought is aesthetic, not scientific. Our thoughts take us to the arts, just as our sensations take us to the sciences.

This is not to say that thoughts are necessarily disordered, or chaotic. Thoughts can and often do exhibit one or another complex order. Sometimes this order is one we establish ourselves, and sometimes it is somehow established for us. I can be obsessed with a series of thoughts, reviewing them over and over. I can descend into neurosis or psychosis.

Yet even the most inflexible thought sequences are subject to revision and dissolution. None of them enjoys the status of reliable scientific consistency found in the world of sensation. In thought, any imaginable sequence can occur. In sensation only some sensible sequences can occur, namely, those consistent with the laws of physics.

Our thoughts, taken in themselves, tend to reduce the logic of representation to a logic of identity. The very freedom of thought allows us to discount all constraint and directly compare the forms displayed by diverse thoughts. The result is a focus on similarities culminating in identities.

In thought, we can afford to disregard what is different and focus on what is the same. We can indulge in the luxury of the pursuit of the forms that interest us while disregarding others which do not. We tend to focus on certain forms, displayed by certain perceptions. Our thoughts, taken alone, push us toward identifying certain particular but independent perceptions which compel us in various ways. (A life of thought is an aesthetic life.)

I can imagine a centaur, or virtually any other creature I please, simply by condensing certain perceptions, or parts of perceptions. This is the thought-logic of assimilation, or identity, where the constraints of fixed relations among perceptions are removed and their free amalgamation in the creation of ever new and exotic perceptions is realized without hindrance.

This capacity of thoughts to be substituted without restriction for one another testifies to the **freedom** of thought, while the inability of sensations to be substituted freely for one another testifies to the **resistance** of sensations.

To substitute any sensation for another requires a measure of work, that is, some excess of force over resistance. Work is never required in thought and always required in sensation. Sensations can be animated only if enough energy is supplied to overcome their resistance. Indeed, energy and resistance are balanced in sensation according to the physical principle of the conservation of energy which does not apply to thought. The bodily bondage of sensation never allows us to disregard physical constraint. Rather than effortlessly comparing perceptions (as we do in thought), we are constrained in sensation to take up perceptions as we encounter them through our bodies.

Being bound to a body in sensation insures an appreciation of how sensations even very similar to one another (say, my body and that of another human being) resist assimilation to identity. Our sensations, taken in themselves, tend to reduce the logic of representation and contrast to a logic of contingency.

In sensation I learn that someone else's body is not my body, that only my body is *my* body, even if there is another body identical to it. It is *my* body that gives me pleasures and pains, and it is the death of *my* body that I must confront unavoidably—other bodies (even that of a twin, if I had one) do not raise these issues for me. It is the very possession of a body that disallows in sensation the luxury of the free pursuit of forms characteristic of thought.

Our bodies force upon us an appreciation of difference, even in the face of sameness, while thought promotes an appreciation of sameness, even in the face of difference. Our bodies teach—by their very presence as conditions of sensation and thought—that we cannot disregard the difference between similarity and sameness. In doing so they suggest the primacy of difference (with contingency as the extreme of difference), just as our thoughts suggest the primacy of sameness (with identity as the extreme of sameness).

Since sensations do not come to us in free and unlimited combinations, but rather in patterned and often predictable patterns of combination, the sensation-logic of contingency promoted by sensations must take these patterns into account. The thought-logic of identity, on the other hand, in admitting all patterns of combination, need take none of them into account. Thus our bodies, and the sensations which they condition, teach us not only that the slightest difference can be fundamental, but also that our sensations are consistently related in certain ways and not in others.

The sensible world on its own testimony stands before us as a sequence of contingent items externally related in specific and reliable ways which can be documented. These items and their external relations are isolated in physics and in the sciences based on physics. Most fundamentally, they include what physicists call matter and energy and their interactions which, taken together constitute the spacetime process that is the physical cosmos.

Our sensations teach us about a world of matter and energy. The perceptions of our physical world turn out to be part of an active course of events, summed up in the natural history of the cosmos, including the process of evolution and the development of life and of our own species, *homo sapiens*.

We call the stability of sensations matter, and their instability (change and motion) energy. Some kinds of sensations, including many atoms and molecules, are highly stable and ubiquitously recurrent, while other atoms and molecules are highly unstable (explosive, radioactive, etc.). Still others, including living creatures, are more or less unique but of limited endurance.

In the natural or physical world there is only matter and energy. Life is understood by science as a function of these, as a biochemical phenomenon. Our bodies teach us of forces and energies which wax and wane through a kaleidoscope of physical manifestations of which our bodies are a small part. Our bodies respond to the world of the senses according to its rules. In the sensation-world every action has a corresponding reaction, and every event a cause. In it there are no original causes or events, no free will, only determination or chance.

Our thoughts, on the other hand, teach us about a world of free will, a world in which thinking is equivalent to doing. The perceptions of our thought-world are mental images, or imaginings, summed up in the non-stop chain of associations of mental images which flood our minds. The constraints of matter and energy are absent in thought, along with the laws of physics. These can be represented in thought, to be sure, and these representations can be variously and fruitfully manipulated, but they themselves do not belong to the thought-world.

We can exercise the will in sensation, but only at the price of labor, whereas our thoughts are bodiless and free of physical constraint. Our thoughts teach us the power to command perceptions as wish-fulfillments, to will perceptions freely. The freedom of will is the ability to substitute, or not to substitute, any perception for any other.

*

Sensations and Thoughts

Normally, our sensations and thoughts constitute ordinary or waking reality, the sum of everyday life since birth. There are, however, sensations and thoughts discontinuous with those of ordinary, waking reality. These other thoughts and sensations constitute a variety of distinct, alternate perceptual realities. They are encountered most commonly when we are asleep, in dreams. But they are also induced to varying degrees by numerous drugs (marijuana, LSD, psychoactive mushrooms, mescaline, etc.) and sometimes occur spontaneously when we are awake (in near-death or out-of-the-body experiences, hallucinations, etc.).

Sensations and thoughts are usually, if not always, combined in these experiences. In dreams, for instance, we often find ourselves with a body and a mind located somewhere unusual, somewhere we do not recognize. But such strange locations usually have recognizable sensations obeying laws similar if not identical to those of ordinary physical reality. I might find myself walking, or running, or swimming, or even somehow flying, etc., and sometimes these activities require effort or labor, just as similar bodily activities do in ordinary, waking reality. At the same time I usually have dream-thoughts accompanying my dream-sensations.

Alternate realities are discontinuous. They are generally unrelated to one another and to ordinary reality, except as parts of our awareness. Alternate realities are distinct packages of thoughts and sensations, distinct from the package we call ordinary reality. Each such package is a perceptual world, an internally bound-up complex exhibiting its own relations, and the sum of these is the content of our awareness.

Dreams and other alternate realities are not thoughts, but alternative complexes of thoughts and sensations. They are strange places in which we repeatedly find ourselves, places different from the place we call ordinary reality. Ordinary reality is distinguished from alternative realities only by its much more consistent and pervasive recurrence, and not by any other factor.

There is a widespread assumption which dismisses alternate realities as oddly (but falsely) compelling thoughts, or hallucinations. Only the false presumption of an 'inner-outer' distinction forces us to classify dreams and other alternate realities as hallucinations.

If we presume the body to be the necessary conduit for what finally comes to us in 'inner' awareness from the 'outside,' then we can understand alternate realities only as a miscellaneous class of falsely-reporting 'perceptions.' Since dreams and other altered states fail to jibe with what the body normally tells us in 'ordinary perception,' they cannot, on this view, be credited with any objective validity. They become instead merely subjective phenomena, emotionally arousing, no doubt, but of no significance about anything outside our own 'inner' states of awareness.

But if we reject the 'inner-outer' distinction as a presupposition of perception, as I propose we do, then thoughts and sensations testifying to apparently alternate realities can be considered seriously as doing just that. Thoughts and sensations can then teach us not only of the world of ordinary reality, but of a series of alternate worlds. This is, of course, consistent with a wide and ancient range of human beliefs in which the testimony of dreams and other extra-ordinary experiences is accepted as valid evidence of alternate realities.

These beliefs are expressed in the ancient religions of the world, including the sorcery or shamanism of many cultures scattered far and wide. They are also found in the mystery religions of later antiquity, in the mysticism of the Sufis and Hindus, in the Hebrew Kaballah, and in the underground traditions of Western magic and occult lore, long repressed by Christianity and scientific naturalism, but never entirely overcome.

It is not necessary to proclaim the validity of all the claims made for alternate realities to recognize that a large body of puzzling and intriguing material variously testifying to such realities exists. The major obstacle to a proper appreciation of this material has been its relegation to the status of hallucination. If it is recognized that 'hallucination' is no more than a stop-gap label for a fictitious 'inner-outer' distinction prejudiced in favor of sensations structured by the body, then the thoughts and sensations encountered in dreams, medita-

Sensations and Thoughts

tion, drug-induced experiences, experiences, epiphanies, and so on, can be taken seriously as evidence of altered states of awareness.

The implication is that there are many worlds, not just one, and a continuity of being, if not always of awareness, far more complex and mysterious than any we allow ourselves to imagine.

A proper recognition of thoughts and sensations as perceptions mitigates against the tendency to reduce either to the terms of the other. To recognize that we are conscious of both thoughts and sensations, and that thoughts are as disembodied as sensations are embodied, is to begin to recognize that consciousness itself lies beyond thought and sensation.

Consciousness has often been identified with the mind rather than the body, but it should be identified with neither. Consciousness is rather to be identified with the soul. As a soul I am neither a thought nor a sensation. Indeed, I am not a perception at all, but rather a capacity to be conscious of perceptions, in addition to being conscious of myself. But because my soul is not a perception, that is, something differentiated that can be represented and contrasted, I literally cannot know *what* I am. I have only the unspecified knowledge *that* I am, and this I call my soul.

CHAPTER FOUR

Solipsism and Behaviorism

Our representational world is made up of perceptions composed of thoughts and sensations. But we often fail to distinguish between them. Like any representation which may be mistaken for what it represents, any sensation may be mistaken for a thought, and any thought for a sensation. We often confuse thoughts and sensations with one another.

These confusions, sustained by the attachments we develop to specific thoughts and sensations, are the major sources of error in human life. The proper understanding of the self is the recognition of the self as a soul, independent of sensations and thoughts. Attachment occurs when we equate our being not with our souls but with some perception, with some sensation or thought.

To confuse souls with perceptions—with sensations and thoughts—is to deny the soul itself. It is to merge the self mistakenly with thoughts or sensations to the point that the self is misunderstood to be no more than a thought or sensation.

The temptation to mis-identify the self with sensations and thoughts is reinforced by the distracting insistence of thoughts and sensations, compared with the mysterious representational opacity of the soul.

The soul is representationally unknown. It can safely be inferred, and perhaps realized in certain meditative or mystical states, but such realizations are arduous, rare, and problematic at best.

Our relative ignorance of the soul, moreover, is compounded by our forceful and vivid, if incomplete, knowledge of sensations and thoughts. The world of sensations and thoughts preeminently imposes itself upon us, and the concerns it raises for us are as varied as they are pressing.

We discover in sensation that we are bodies and in thought that we are minds, and these seem more immediately telling and sufficient candidates for self-identification than the elusive soul, of which we seem to know only that it is neither a sensation nor a thought.

Our mis-identifications of self with body and mind are mutually self-perpetuating. Since bodies and minds are radically discontinuous, neither can explain the discontinuity between them. Each can only try to swallow the other, and thus to deny any discontinuity between sensations and thoughts. The only way to sustain such a denial is to insist either that thoughts are in fact sensations, or that sensations are in fact thoughts. The dualism promises to disappear if minds can be reduced to bodies, or bodies to minds.

*

I call someone who confuses sensations with thoughts (bodies with minds) a solipsist. A solipsist holds that sensations are thoughts; that sensations are actually mental images. And I call someone who makes the opposite error, who confuses thoughts with sensations (minds with bodies), a behaviorist.

For the solipsist, the ultimate reality is thought: the unconditional ability to freely substitute one perception for another. For the behaviorist, the ultimate reality is sensation, where the substitution of sensations for one another is never unrestricted but always highly conditioned.

If all perceptions are sensations, as the behaviorist supposes, then any thought must be a sensation, something that in principle can be seen, heard, etc. A behaviorist holds that thoughts are physical phenomena: hormones, electrical impulses in the brain, etc.

Solipsism and Behaviorism

If all perceptions are thoughts, as the solipsist supposes, then to 'see' the conditions of sight, to 'hear' the conditions of hearing, and so on, must somehow be to think thoughts. A solipsist holds that sensations are not physical phenomena, but thoughts in the mind.

Solipsism is self-absorption in thought. The solipsist can think of himself only as a thought. His task is to find himself in a thought, and the only thought in which he can find himself is some kind of thought of himself thinking.

Since there is no thought of thinking—as we saw in the last chapter—the solipsist's search for himself as a thinking thought is ultimately futile. Thinking is the movement of thought, the free substitution of thoughts for one another. Although thinking is endlessly displayed by thought, it is never thought as such.

The solipsist's pseudo-thought of himself thinking is the pseudo-thought of his freely substituting thoughts for one another. It is the pseudo-thought of his will. The will, insofar as it is omnipotent in thought, inspires the solipsistic idea of God, including man as God. The solipsist presumes himself to be all-powerful, or godlike, even if he can never quite succeed in finding a thought of himself thinking.

The behaviorist, on the other hand, can sense himself only as a sensation. Behaviorism is self-absorption in sensation. The behaviorist's task is to find himself in a sensation, and the only sensation in which he can find himself is the sensation of his own physical body.

Unlike the solipsist, who can never find himself in thought, the behaviorist clearly and unambiguously finds himself in the sensation of his body. But he learns from his body not the exciting news that he is potentially omnipotent, but the sobering news that he is all too finite: a dependent, limited creature destined—in spite of transient pleasures—to suffer and die.

The behaviorist recognizes only what he takes to be public sensations. He can recognize himself only in a sensation, and most obviously in the sensation of his own body. Behaviorism introduces the idea of nature. Although the behaviorist identifies self with nature, or the body, the body is merely a location in the world of sensation whose survival is a matter of chance and determinism.

The exercise of the will, so important to the solipsist, is an illusion to the behaviorist. For him all perceptions are patterned in accordance with the laws of physics, where an expense of energy is always the price of action.

For the behaviorist, all perceptions are sensations, which are either chance or determined. And neither chance nor determinism is free. The randomness of chance is the prison of the arbitrary, and the dead weight of determinism is inexorability itself. Chance and determinism are the products of the behaviorist's content and form dualism. Chance is the random chaos of disorder, or content, and determinism is the rigid patterned sequence of order, or form.

Since there is no thought which shows someone else having a thought, the solipsist imagines that the physical world must somehow be his private thought. Public physical perceptions (sensations) are to him as much illusions as his own soul.

That there are other bodies like his own which do not offer him their "inner side," as does his own body, remains for the solipsist a curiosity. He denies that the bodies of others have any "inner side," and insists that they are items reserved for his private contemplation.

Since there are sensations (our bodies) which show that sensations are seen, heard, etc., the behaviorist sees (hears, etc.) the world only as a series of public perceptions, or sensations. To him private perceptions are as much illusions as his own soul.

That he seems to possess a private realm of thoughts seems to the behaviorist a curious physiological effect. He insists that his thoughts are physical perceptions which, in principle, can be shared with others. Perhaps, he might say, some sort of scientific apparatus will someday survey his (or anyone's) most "private thoughts" so as to reveal them to be the public sensations (electric impulses, brain waves, etc.) he claims they really are.

Solipsism and Behaviorism

*

The subjugation of sensations to thoughts in solipsism is their subjugation to a pseudo-logic of identity, to a belief that all perceptions must be (like thoughts) private, mental wholes identified by the forms they display as wholes, not the roles they play as parts.

The subjugation of thoughts to sensations in behaviorism is their subjugation to a pseudo-logic of contingency, to a belief that all perceptions must be (like sensations) public, physical parts distinguished by the roles they play as parts, not the wholes they display.

*

Consider first the solipsist's pseudo-logic of identity.

We have seen that the mind is quite free in its range of association. In the mind we can substitute virtually any thought for any other. There is no obstacle in thought to the conflation (and pseudo-identification) of thoughts that are merely similar, or even different, from one another.

This is the power displayed in imagination, or fantasy. In imaginative fantasy, where various thoughts are freely substituted for one another, it is easy to take our more compelling thoughts as standards by which other less compelling thoughts are identified and conflated together.

It works this way: If one thing reminds me of another by similarity or even mere relational association, I am inclined to mis-identify them. Similarity and difference collapse into pseudo-identity as soon as I conflate thoughts that are merely similar and different. And it is the free substitution of thoughts for one another that allows me to treat similarities and differences *as if* they were identities.

To act solipsistically, to treat sensations as if they were thoughts, is to compound this pseudo-logic of identity, extending it from our thoughts to our sensations, that is, to all perception.

Sensations treated in this way become resonant, or symbolically empowered archetypes. Physical objects and events—the bones of a saint, the holiday ritual, the flag, the work of art, etc.—are swept up into the fantasy. Such sensations become sacred exemplars to which other more or less approximate sensations are assimilated, and thereby sacralized.

Thus umbrellas, lampposts, bananas, cigars, and many other similar sensations can be made symbolically equivalent to penises by treating them as identical to penises. So too can the experiences of daily life be sacralized through identification with similar experiences described in the Bible, the Koran, stories of the Buddha, etc.

This process of using an archetype, a privileged example, as a standard for other perceptions I call symbolization. Symbolization insists upon an enforced equivalence among less than identical perceptions. The pseudo-logic of symbolizing identification confounds representation itself. It insists that even perceptions non-identical to the exemplar be included in the equation of identity, a point well illustrated in a passage from Johan Huizinga's *The Waning of the Middle Ages*.

In the chapter entitled "Symbolism in Decline," Huizinga writes that in medieval times "religious emotion always tended to be transmuted into images. Mystery seemed to become graspable by the mind when invested with a perceptible form. The need of adoring the ineffable in visible shapes was continually creating ever new figures. In the fourteenth century, the cross and the lamb no longer sufficed for the effusions of overflowing love offered to Jesus; to these is added the adoration of the name of Jesus, which occasionally threatens to eclipse even that of the cross. Henry Suso tattoos the name of Jesus over his heart and compares himself to the lover who wears the name of his beloved embroidered on his coat. Bernardino of Siena, at the end of a moving sermon, lights two candles and shows the multitude a board a yard in length, bearing on an azure ground the name of Jesus in golden letters surrounded by the sun's rays. The people filling the church kneel down and weep with emotion."

Whatever his reference to the "ineffable" may mean, Huizinga is talking about thoughts in my sense of mental images. As he makes plain, the literal name of Jesus—itself a bare sound with little if any representational capacity vis-a-vis the life of Jesus—nonetheless can be so closely identified with Jesus so as to be incorporated among the other images which have been combined together to symbolize the life of Jesus.

In a the full course of the pseudo-logic of identity, the person and life of Jesus are fused even with the physical expression of his name, as painted on a board in gold letters. The name is purported to be identical with his person and life, so that to confront the former is literally to confront the latter. And the people knelt down and wept.

*

Next consider the behaviorist's pseudo-logic of contingency:

The behaviorist stands as alter-ego to the solipsist, opposing him at every point. Instead of treating sensations as thoughts, he treats thoughts as sensations. This is to apply the pseudo-logic of contingency, characteristic of sensations, to thoughts.

It works like this: Sensations lend themselves to an over-appreciation of difference in similarity. The difference displayed in similarity plays a vital role in the world of sensation. One sensible perception may be quite similar to another, yet be quite useless for some given task or purpose, while the other is just what is required. Of two otherwise identical but slightly different sized wrenches, for instance, only one can remove the bolt necessary to change a tire.

This is precisely the situation glossed over so effortlessly in the fantasy of thought, where any thought can be substituted for any other. In sensation, no sensation can be substituted freely for any other. The distinction is crucial. To substitute perceptions for one another freely (as in thought) is to affirm their interchangeability, and by implication, some kind of identity among them. But not to be able to substitute perceptions for one another freely (as in sensation) is to affirm their non-interchangeability, and by implication, some kind of difference among them.

The behaviorist is overly impressed by our manifest inability to freely interchange perceptions—an inability demonstrated over and over again in sensation. In sensation, all substitutions, save of pure identities for pure identities, are sooner or later shown to be incomplete.

I can substitute honey for sugar in my tea, but even if my taste buds are deceived certain chemical tests will reveal the difference by some further contrast of sensation, and thus mark the limits of that substitution. Or I might substitute your car for mine, and although it might do many things indistinguishably from mine (say, go sixty miles per hour), it will also do many things differently (say, take longer to start). Such tests probing for differences are characteristic of the sciences, and taking them seriously reflects the scientific bent of the behaviorist.

Since all perceptions, save the purest identities (e.g., H_2O), are believed by the behaviorist to be revealed sooner or later as differences, he mistakenly concludes that similarity is fundamentally the testimony of difference, that perceptions are different unless identical.

Sensations, under the behaviorist's pseudo-logic of contingency, are dissimilated on the basis of the forms they fail to share in common. Similarity collapses into contingency. All representations save identities are ignored. All perceptions except identities are mis-classified as different from one another.

*

The solipsist makes the opposite mistake from the behaviorist. He assumes that all perceptions are interchangeable, that sooner or later any perception can stand in relation to any other, that similarity is fundamentally the testimony of sameness.

If any perception can stand in relation to any other, then the relations between perceptions are unproblematic. And if the relations between perceptions are unproblematic, they are of little concern. The solipsist is free to attend to perceptions, no matter how they are related to one another. He can follow them simply as representations.

Solipsism and Behaviorism

The behaviorist, on the other hand, assumes that all perceptions are not interchangeable; that no perception can stand in relation to any and all others. If no perception can stand in relation to any and all others, then the relations between perceptions becomes the paramount concern.

According to the behaviorist pseudo-logic of contingency, perceptions are sorted out on the basis of their relational compatibility, or incompatibility, and on that basis alone. The behaviorist is not free, like the solipsist, to attend merely to those perceptions he wishes to relate together, to his fantasies. Rather he must concentrate on the effort of isolating those already related perceptions which press upon him.

*

The solipsist, for whom all relations are possible, takes perceptions as things, as objects and events. To take a perception as a thing is to attend to the relations displayed by its constituent perceptions (its internal relations), while ignoring those into which it enters with other perceptions (its external relations).

Since he can follow perceptions however they are arranged, what strikes the solipsist is the product of any such arrangement: the perception in itself, its internal relations. The solipsist everywhere sees parts as wholes. For him all relations are internal relations. External relations are admitted only insofar as they are taken as internal relations.

The behaviorist, committed to the notion that all relations are not possible, takes perceptions not as things but as relations. To take a perception as a relation is to attend to the role it plays in some more inclusive perception (its external relations), while ignoring the relations displayed by its constituent perceptions (its internal relations).

Since he cannot rearrange perceptions as he pleases, what strikes the behaviorist is the problem of rearranging them, of their external relations. From his perspective, all relations become external relations. Internal relations are admitted only insofar as they can be taken as external relations. The behaviorist everywhere sees wholes as parts. And he sees parts, which cannot have internal relations, as points.

Perceptions viewed behavioristically come to be defined by the criteria not of the forms they display individually, as in solipsism, but by those they help to display collectively; they are defined not by their wholeness, but by their partness, their external relations.

The external relations of perceptions, abstracted from the actual perceptions that display them, are simply patterns. Patterns may be vague, elusive, and obscure, on the one hand, or clear, precise, and obvious, on the other. They can be trivial or profound, narrow or broad, straightforward or subtle.

The most rigorous patterns are the laws of nature, say Newton's inverse square law, or Einstein's $E = mc^2$. Trivial examples are "water runs downhill" and "day follows night."

Patterns are refined by abstraction, by comparing them in terms of what they share in common. Abstraction is the behaviorist's counterpart to the symbolization of the solipsist. Abstractions are reifications: generalizations as likely as not to be paradoxical and self-contradictory.

*

For the behaviorist to take thoughts as sensations is to ignore how thoughts differ from sensations, just as for the solipsist to take sensations as thoughts is to ignore how sensations differ from thoughts.

The solipsist represses sensations by pretending they are thoughts, and the behaviorist represses thoughts by pretending they are sensations. Repression is not wholesale denial, but selective distortion and displacement.

Behaviorism ignores what Freud called the primary processes in favor of what he called the secondary processes, while solipsism does the reverse.

Insofar as Freud was a behaviorist, he was a scientist intent upon explaining the primary processes in terms of the secondary processes. Insofar as he was a solipsist, he was an artist intent upon displaying the secondary processes as refined displays of the primary processes.

For the solipsist, sensations function unconsciously. For the behaviorist, thoughts function unconsciously. The solipsist is conscious only of thoughts, the behaviorist only of sensations.

I can be solipsistically enthralled by the wholeness of a perception, and proceed to symbolize it by comparison with other perception-wholes, ignoring its partness. Or I can be behavioristically impressed by the partness of a perception, and proceed to abstract it by comparison with other perception-parts, ignoring its wholeness.

I can almost effect a kind of left brain-right brain simultaneity and virtually do both at once. But even so I can be conscious at any moment only of one or the other—of sensations as thoughts or of thoughts as sensations—no matter how much or how quickly I shift between them. In the same way, I can be conscious of Wittgenstein's famous duck-rabbit drawing only as a duck or a rabbit, but never of both at once, no matter how much or how quickly I can shift between them.

Symbolization is the repressive mechanism of solipsism, and abstraction is the repressive mechanism of behaviorism. Patterned relations displayed by repressed sensations in solipsism are denied. Patterned relations not displayed by repressed thoughts in behaviorism are imposed upon them.

*

Archetypes are the criteria by which the solipsist picks and chooses, an archetype being some specific perception whose internal relations, or forms, strike the solipsist as especially compelling. To recognize an archetype is to initiate the process of symbolization outlined above: the identification of similar and even different perceptions with the archetype in question.

The difficulty is that compounding more or less similar perceptions with archetypes, along with other dissimilar but related perceptions, inevitably waters down the original archetype. The less-than-identical perceptions continue to differ from the archetype with which they are presumed to be identical. When the compelling impulse of the original archetypal exemplar is blurred and diluted to the point where it is overwhelmed and lost, then the pseudo-logic of identity is dissolved, and the world of the solipsist dissolves.

Huizinga, in the same chapter of *The Waning of the Middle Ages*, provides us with an account of the dissolution of symbolism from late medieval times: "Finding symbols and allegories had become a meaningless intellectual pastime, shallow fancifulness resting on a single analogy. The sanctity of the object still gives it some small spiritual value. As soon as the craze of symbolism spreads to profane or simply moral matters, decadence is manifest. Froissart, in *Li orloge amoureus*, compares all the details of love to the various parts of a timepiece. Chastellain and Molinet vie with each other in political symbolism. The three estates represent the qualities of the virgin. The seven electors of the Empire signify the virtues; the five towns of Artois and Hainout, which in 1477 remained faithful to the house of Burgundy, are the five virgins. In reality this is symbolism turned upside down; it uses things of the higher order as symbols of things of the lower order, for these authors in effect raise terrestrial things to the higher level by employing sacred conceptions merely to adorn them."

What Huizinga calls "symbolism turned upside down" is the dissolution of symbolism. The more perceptions are brought into the process, the more arbitrary and mechanical it becomes, the more likely it is to end in decadence and scepticism.

Huizinga's examples should not imply that we have to do with an archaic or primitive phenomenon confined to some remote past. One glance at television advertising or political propaganda in our own time will dispel that illusion.

*

The behaviorist, on the other hand, presupposes that the resistance of sensations to mutual free substitution extends to all of his perceptions, including his thoughts. The behaviorist sustains his presupposition that thoughts are sensations, in spite of the mental evidence of the free substitution of perceptions in thought, by regarding thoughts as a random or predetermined series of illusory perceptions.

This clears the way for the unrestricted mis-application of the pseudo-logic of contingency to all perceptions, to thoughts as well as sensations. The behaviorist ends by treating all perceptions as if they were contingent to one another. He disregards their internal relations and the comparisons of internal relations that arise out of their sameness, similarity, and difference. His question, given any two perceptions, is not how they stand vis-a-vis one another on the spectrum of representation and contrast, but whether or not they stand in some relation to one another, and if so, in which relation or relations.

This attitude is scientific, just as the solipsist's attitude is aesthetic. The scientist's preoccupation with formal regularities is nothing other than the behaviorist's preoccupation with the relations among perceptions. The scientist's theory, hypothesis, or law is the behaviorist's paradigm.

Like the behaviorist, the scientist recognizes only that perceptions are identical with themselves and contingent to all other perceptions. The scientific behaviorist does not recognize the other aspects of representation and contrast intrinsic to perceptions: pictures, functions, kinds, and the rest. His ontology recognizes only self-identical objects standing in contrast to other self-identical objects.

The further the behaviorist-scientist sifts perceptions in search of slighter and slighter differences, the fewer perceptions survive to count as identical even to themselves. Even so-called pure substances, such as water or gold, are rarely found in an absolutely pure state (although such a state can be approximated).

The behaviorist world, for almost all practical purposes, becomes a world of contingent items variously related to one another. In this state, the internal relations of perceptions, their thinghood, is boiled down to the vanishing point. The behaviorist's preoccupation with external relations leads to a disregard of internal relations. Perceptions as things finally end as mere intersections of relations, or points.

*

An apple, for example, is never for the behaviorist a specific discrete display of internal relations, but always a point in a network of relations among other points of reference. An apple is a fruit; it grows on certain trees at certain times and places; it can be picked, stored, transported, bought and sold, eaten, and so on. Whatever can enter into these and other relevant external relations becomes an apple.

The apple has internal relations as well: it has color, a shape; it can be cut up, revealing fleshy fruit, a core with seeds, etc. But these internal relations become, for the behaviorist, external relations. Color, shape, fleshy fruit, etc., are finally taken by the behaviorist to be points in a network of relations. As a result, nothing intrinsic about the apple is left. Rather everything becomes extrinsic. Everything is derived in terms of factors beyond the apple itself, from its partness.

The apple finally becomes an illusion, a bundle of qualities or properties which are themselves illusions, the function of certain other relationships, usually mathematically expressed. The redness of the apple becomes nothing more than the mathematical formula for the wave-length of red light, which in turn becomes a function of still further relations, say nuclear forces, also mathematically expressed, and so on to the edge of physics.

For the solipsist, on the other hand, an apple is precisely the specific network of internal relations that it is, a view that deflates external relations into internal ones. The solipsist does not care how the apple itself is related to anything else, nor how any of its parts, as parts, are related to any others. If he is concerned with the apple, he is concerned with its internal relations alone, with the forms it displays. If he is concerned with a part of the apple, he is concerned with the internal relations of that part, with the forms that part displays; and so on.

*

The solipsist recognizes sameness and similarity among perceptions, and substitutes perceptions for one another accordingly. What he ignores are the external relations among perceptions. He ignores the

Solipsism and Behaviorism

question of whether or not perceptions can be related in favor of the question of the forms displayed by those perceptions which concern him.

The solipsist is indifferent to the constraints on our ability to relate perceptions. That many perceptions are related only in certain ways and not in others is not itself a perception that can function as a symbolic archetype. It finds no place in the solipsist's ontology.

The behaviorist, by taking internal relations as external relations, erases anything that could distinguish them as internal relations. His world loses all depth, becoming a sort of ontological flat land. That perceptions represent one another to varying degrees is declared an illusion and dismissed.

Paradigms effectively reduce perceptions to their external relations. Although internal relations are always the external relations of other perceptions, what counts in behaviorism is no particular display of forms in a particular perception (no particular birch tree, for instance), but the generalized, more or less consistently repeated patterns found again and again (the generalized concept or type of all birch trees).

By privileging external relations, the behaviorist places them beyond criticism. They become standards of criticism (and of truth, value, inference, etc.). Just as the synthetic process of symbolism in the long run undermines its own exemplars, so the analytic process of abstraction in the long run undermines its own paradigms.

*

To the behaviorist, the positing of independent, criteriological concepts is the only way to give any adequate account of our experience. Concepts are the stock in trade of modern behavioristic philosophy and so-called critical thinking. The modern behaviorist—the modernist—presumes that concepts are somehow self-conceptualizing, and that sensations are somehow intersections of concepts.

Applying the pseudo-logic of contingency to what he takes to be sensations, the behaviorist concludes that forms are separable from the instances of their display. He identifies thoughts with forms and sensations with the content of forms. This pseudo-logic of contingency recognizes and isolates recurring forms distributed across many perceptions. This reification of forms separates them from the perceptions which display them, and sets them up (falsely) as axiomatic criteria.

It is but a short step to mis-identifying those recurring forms with thoughts, and their contents (their specific, individual points of intersection) with sensations. Thoughts for the behaviorist become not what they are, but a reification of abstract conceptualization, and sensations become not what they are, but the raw, disorganized, manifold of sensuous (physical) intuition, the stuff (content) which is subjected to conceptualization (order). Hence the false epistemology of Western ideology, first developed by the ancient Greeks.

For example, to substitute different horses for one another in the same relations (saddled and ridden, fed and brushed, pulling a wagon, grazing in a pasture, etc.) is to produce the common, generalized residue of horse: the empirical concept of horseness. This concept of horseness is the schema of those external relations into which individual horses (and their individual parts) normally enter. It is the generalized totality of roles they (and their parts) usually play.

By the same token, a horse can be purely a sensation only insofar as it is specifically and individually manifest: *this* horse at *this* time doing *just* what he is doing. A sensation on this view becomes a "something" not yet conceptualized, not yet specified in terms of its possible roles, and hence not yet a "horse" at all. Indeed, sensations so construed ('pure' sensations) are fleeting, inarticulated moments, a chaos perhaps real enough to be felt, but too elusive to be defined.

A series of familiar dichotomies blends into this behaviorist distinction between form and content. Sensations are characterized as subjective particulars, concepts as objective universals, and so on. The question of how such particular, subjective chaotic contents can be mediated by such universal, objective, orderly forms is the pseudo-problem behavioristic Western philosophy has set for itself.

Solipsism and Behaviorism

*

The solipsist, who applies the pseudo-logic of identity to what he takes to be thoughts, arrives at a very different outcome. For him, forms are rooted in the very perceptions that display them, so that form and content are always inseparable. They are inseparable not only in the sense that there can be no forms if there are no perceptions to display them, but also in the sense that each display of forms requires just those perceptions that actually display them.

The solipsist rejects the behavioristic notion that the same or similar forms can be displayed by different perceptions. He holds instead that any re-display of the same or similar forms can only be a re-display of the same perception.

The solipsist is not tempted to mis-identify forms with thoughts, nor content with sensations. He errs in another direction: he is unable to distinguish at all—even mistakenly—between thoughts and sensations. Since thoughts and sensations are contingent to one another, they cannot be indistinguishable. Yet the pseudo-logic of identity, by counting similarity as identity, allows itself the pretense of identifying sensations with thoughts.

The solipsist does not create for himself a philosophical dualism of order and chaos like the behaviorist. Rather he creates a spurious hyperunity of perceptions, a fantasy into which the world is condensed.

Behaviorism is objective (public) but alienating: order and chaos are abstract alternatives from which the real thought-and-sensation content has been drained. If chaos is the content of order, as the behaviorist presupposes, it is an empty, pseudo-content, even though it provides, as far as it goes, an accurate map of the general, external relations of the world.

Solipsism, on the other hand, is subjective (private) but enthralling. The solipsist allows himself to be indulged, but at the price of objectivity. His exemplars are powerful, but they offer no realistic guide to the structure of the world. They are myths.

*

Some paradigms, like some archetypes, are more resistant and durable than others. The life of Jesus as an archetype, and Newtonian mechanics as a paradigm, have, in spite of numerous qualifications, each long retained a widespread command of belief. Yet each breaks down at significant points, frustrating our dogmatic appraisals.

The scepticism which inevitably arises out of both solipsism and behaviorism lies in the gap between an exhaustive ideal (the entirely adequate archetype or paradigm) and our inability to sustain and generalize such an ideal. The psychologies of behaviorism and solipsism run on parallel lines: promise and anticipation, struggle, success and euphoria, problems and second thoughts, doubt and hope, and either resignation and despair, or new promise and anticipation, and so on.

*

Solipsism arises out of art, and behaviorism out of science.

The solipsist, treating sensations as thoughts, follows the impulse of the artist in emphasizing the free substitution of perceptions for one another. The behaviorist, treating thoughts as sensations, follows the impulse of the scientist in emphasizing the recalcitrant patterning of facts.

The artist wishes to create, and creation is possible only insofar as perceptions can be freely manipulated. The scientist wishes to learn, and learning is possible only insofar as perceptions display a consistent patterning.

The scientist becomes a behaviorist at the point where he presumes that all perceptions are patterned as they are preeminently in sensation, that indeed all perceptions *are* sensations. The artist becomes a solipsist when he presumes that all perceptions are malleable as they are preeminently in thought, that indeed all perceptions *are* thoughts.

The artistic impulse, taken to its solipsistic extreme, produces religion, and the scientific impulse, taken to its behavioristic extreme, produces ideology. Religion and ideology are the social expressions of solipsism and behaviorism, and they are as old as stone age rituals and calculations.

The notion that religion somehow precedes ideology as an earlier, more primitive stage of human consciousness is a misleading ideological prejudice. Solipsistic religion and behavioristic ideology both are as old and as new as the human condition.

Even though the word 'ideology,' compared to the word 'religion,' is a relatively recent term (dating from the period of the French Revolution), we find evidence of the ideological outlook paralleling the religious impulse throughout human history. We see it in the ancient materialism of Lucretius, Epicurus, and Democritus, and even earlier in the naturalistic sentiments of Egyptian and Mesopotamian texts. There is even prehistoric evidence of the human ideological disposition (cf. Alexander Marshack's *The Roots of Civilization*).

Although religion and ideology go back to the beginnings of human history, their competition is complex and uneven. Its course in the Western world can briefly be summarized. There was a long period in antiquity, roughly the thousand years or so from the sixth and fifth centuries BC to the third or fourth centuries AD, when the cosmopolitan rationalism expressed in Greek philosophy and science and Roman organization and engineering dominated (without destroying) the religious impulses then expressed in mystery religions and paganism.

With the rise of Christianity and Islam, this ideological era ended. For the next thousand years—the middle ages—the tables were reversed, with new religions dominating the surviving ideological remnants of antiquity. With the European Renaissance, however, the balance shifted again in favor of ideological preoccupations, which we usually lump under the label of modernism.

Since about the fifteenth century, various modernist ideologies associated with science, technology, and commerce have gradually come to dominate Western civilization, while the traditional religions, particularly Christianity, have been increasingly rent by division and controversy. The watershed of this cultural transition in the West was probably the nineteenth century. The religious impulse has survived, of course, in spite of the Enlightenment's devastating ideological attack upon it as myth and superstition. In romanticism, the arts, and the popular media we have seen a virtual rebirth of paganism, even as the great modernist ideologies have continued to define most of Western culture.

The point is not so much that one era is more religious and another more ideological, as that religion and ideology continually coexist in an ongoing competition neither can win or lose, though one or the other sometimes appears on the verge of doing so. Just as the cult of Dionysius and the mysteries of Isis coexisted with the ancient Academy and Lycium, so today do born again Christians coexist with secular academicians and rocket scientists.

*

The essence of religion is the creation of the sacred, the vehicle of which is solipsistic symbolization. The sacred is the condensed archetype, the over-determined exemplar, asserted as the standard for perceptual judgment. What distinguishes any religion is precisely the assertion of such an archetype, the recognition and embrace of which is the test of that religion, its ritual. To be a Christian I must accept the divinity of Christ, that is, Christ as a privileged archetype, as the unique vehicle of my salvation. The Christian holds that it is only through his or her acceptance of Christ that redemption is possible. It is the same for all organized religions, from Judaism to Hinduism to Shintoism. In each case, some verbal formula or ritualistic act affirming the archetype in question, some test of faith, defines who is, and who is not, included in the religion.

Religion does not have to be organized to be effective. Indeed, the process of solipsistic symbolization occurs spontaneously, in many settings, most of them not what we would ordinarily consider religious. Style, fashion, propaganda, advertising, the performing arts, politics, and many other everyday social and cultural activities derive their main force from solipsistic symbolization. These contemporary solipsistic symbolizations may not have behind them the traditional authority of an organized church or religion, but their influence may be just as pervasive, perhaps even more so, especially where supported by the power of the state. Endlessly rebroadcast television commercials promote archetypal identifications just as effectively as the endlessly repeated Catholic mass, or the endlessly repeated pledge of allegiance to the flag.

This kind of religiosity has become a hallmark of modern times. It is religion divorced from church and scripture. One of its first expressions was romanticism, the reassertion, beginning in the eighteenth century, of the archetypal religious power of natural phenomena, of landscapes, seacapes, and especially of the beauty and sublimity displayed not only in nature but in our mental ability to rehearse and compound natural images into art: into poetry and literature, music and painting.

With traditional religion in the West reeling under the Enlightenment indictment, art rose up in the 19th century to fill the gap. This new art proliferated into a spectrum ranging from highbrow forms (like opera and symphonic music) to middlebrow sentimentalism (like Dickens' novels) to lowbrow entertainment and advertising (like the Sears Roebuck catalogue). Not all these solipsistic expressions could claim the kind of widespread disciplined allegiance characteristic of, say, Christianity, but all could claim to offer at least limited epiphanies, transcendent moments or extra-sensory intimations, which suggested, at least, the existence of a redemptive spiritual realm.

The most potent of these secular, romantic religions—those that generated the widespread disciplined allegiance characteristic of Christianity—were nationalism and racism. Nationalism has been as often as not the major modern expression of racism. The nation, after all, has usually meant 'the people,' and 'the people' has usually meant the predominant group, the core race. No longer able to find salvation in Christ, many Western peoples have opted to find it in their racial-national ethos. Racism is a form of ancestor worship. The physical type of the ancestors, and their cultural achievements, are symbolically rendered mystical and sacred, a mysterious font of energy through which the qualified individual finds a redemptive extra-individual catharsis.

*

The essence of ideology, on the other hand, is abstract knowledge, the generalization of patterned relations. Ideology displays no sacred supercharged archetype, but rules and categories, classifications and concepts, detached from specific instances and abstracted into a rule or law. The ideological outlook is secular and materialistic rather than sacred and spiritual.

Ideology does not promise the kind of sweeping redemption characteristic of religion, but a practical realism aimed at materialistic survival. There is no salvation here, strictly speaking, but rather a kind of practical efficacy. The ideologue relies on a rationalized pattern of experience, an abstract system detached from its original, concrete manifestations and applied generically as a reified, universal rule.

The denial of solipsistic salvation leaves ideologues confined within the material world of sensation. Unable to promise redemption after death, ultimately having to accept death, ideologues can only promise a kind of displaced redemption on earth. The redemptive impulse, its traditional spiritual goal repressed, is ironically expressed as a transformation of the physical world. Salvation is not to be in any fuzzy hereafter, but in a concrete future here on earth. This future—envisioned along the entire ideological gamut from communism to capitalism—is an idealized physical life of convenience and pleasure—consumerism—with pain and drudgery removed.

*

Religions and ideologies have dominated the historical record, at the price of much intolerance and violence. As long as the standard of reality is held to be some archetype or paradigm, this will continue. Even the mutual recognition of religion and ideology we call postmodernism only confirms, and does not transcend, our enthrallment with archetypes and paradigms. It signifies a disillusioned but resigned weariness born of inconclusive struggle.

There have always been those, however, who have resisted the dominant dogmatisms of their times, not by appeal to yet another dogmatism, but by resistance to the attachments of their perceptions. The point is not to deny perceptions their due, but to recognize their incompleteness, their dependence on something non-perceptual, on the soul.

CHAPTER FIVE

Signs

The stipulations made in the previous chapters about perceptions, and the consequences drawn from those stipulations, can be illustrated by considering how we use certain perceptions as signs for other perceptions. This chapter constitutes a demonstration, rather technical in nature, of the possibilities of signification inherent in our perceptions. The next chapter will explore language as a system of perceptual signs. Once the perceptual basis of signification and language is clarified, we will be in a position to appreciate how we can speak (or not speak) about the non-perceptual soul.

*

A sign is a substitute for what it signifies; it goes proxy for it. All signs are perceptions, and they signify other perceptions, or the forms displayed by perceptions, or the comparisons of such forms, or any or all of these. Insofar as signs signify perceptions they are **names**, and names (except pictographs) do not represent but consistently contrast with the perceptions they signify. Insofar as signs consistently contrast with the forms displayed by otherwise differing perceptions, they are **punctuations**. And insofar as signs signify the comparison of forms displayed by perceptions, they are **values**. Values are judgments comparing perceptions. Names signify perceptions, punctuations signify forms (that is, relations among perceptions), and values signify comparisons of forms displayed by perceptions.

A name can be either a representation (an icon) or a contrast (a label), or some mixture thereof. Names which represent perceptions (like pictographs) signify them simply by representing them. But most names signify perceptions by standing in some consistently contrasting or labelling relation to them, at least samples of which can be represented. A photograph of my son signifies him by representing him. His name signifies him, not by representing him, but by standing in a consistently contrasting relation to him, instances of which I can represent, say on a videotape.

To signify not perceptions but the forms displayed by perceptions, or the comparison of such forms, a sign can neither contrast with nor represent those forms and comparisons. Forms and comparisons, though displayed by perceptions, are not themselves perceptions, and so cannot be represented or contrasted by perceptions. Nor can a sign be related to any forms or comparison of forms it signifies, for signs (as perceptions) can be related only to other perceptions. The punctuation of forms and the evaluation of comparisons has nothing to do with representation, contrast, or relation among perceptions.

To signify forms by punctuation is to mark out their display through a variety of otherwise differing perceptions. Forms can be punctuated only insofar as they are consistently displayed by perceptions. It is the forms perceptions display, not perceptions as such, that are punctuated by signs. To signify values is to mark out comparisons that arise out of the representation and contrast of perceptions. As an evaluation a sign signifies not the perceptions displaying the forms compared, but the comparison of the forms displayed by those perceptions. Yet punctuation is not evaluation; forms are not comparisons.

Representation and contrast make comparison possible. Comparisons are relative (not relational) aspects of representation and contrast. The general modes of representation and contrast (identities, replicas, pictures, varieties, and the rest) are comparisons, but there are many other, more limited comparisons as well. We have seen that the general representational modes constitute a logic applicable to all perceptions. Identity, replication, picturing, and the rest, are ways in which all perceptions must stand vis-a-vis one another simply by virtue of representing and contrasting with one another. All other comparisons presuppose these. But that one perception is original, or better, or uglier, or heavier, or darker, or lower, etc., depends on how it compares to certain other perceptions with regard to the specific forms that are displayed by each, and to the specific configurations of those forms.

To compare forms is not to relate them, although relations are what are being compared (that is, sets of internal relations displayed by perceptions), and forms that are compared have to be related (by relating the perceptions that display them). To relate perceptions to one another, and so the forms they display, is not in itself to draw any comparison between those forms. A comparison can be drawn only when we can already appreciate that the perceptions in question represent or contrast with one another. Comparison is possible only on the basis of representation and contrast.

To claim, for example, that perception X is more beautiful than perception Y presupposes that the forms displayed by X are the same, similar, or different from those displayed by Y. I must be able to make this comparison before I can advance the claim that X is more (or less) beautiful than Y, for representation and contrast are what allow me to recognize (and specify) those formal details, present in X and not in Y, whose testimony is the only proof I can cite that X is more (or less) beautiful than Y. Such representation and contrast is independent of (but not opposed to) any relation between X and Y. I call signs signifying comparisons values since every comparison evaluates perceptions vis-a-vis one another on the basis of the forms they display.

The substitution of perceptions for perceptions, or for the forms other perceptions display, or for the comparisons of those forms, constitute the modes of signification. To the extent to which a dollar bill (or the visual mark $, or an entry in my checkbook, or a credit card, or something costing a dollar, or the thought of any of these, etc.) is substituted for other dollar bills, it signifies those other dollar bills. Signification takes place when one perception is put in place of (and for) another perception, or in place of (and for) certain forms or certain comparisons among forms.

I notice that lightning is related to (and so already substitutes for) thunder, although I find it too unwieldy a substitute for me to command. I (not being Zeus) cannot conveniently signify thunder by lightning. I can, however, conveniently substitute a representation of lightning both for the lightning itself as well as for a representation of thunder (which I have already substituted for the thunder itself). That is, I cannot signify thunder by lightning but I can signify a perception signifying thunder by a perception signifying lightning. I use thoughts to signify thunder and lightning, but I might also use convenient physical perceptions, for example, visual marks or spoken sounds, to do the same thing.

When I notice certain forms displayed by a variety of perceptions, I can signify them only by virtue of substituting for them some perception. I can see many triangles displayed by many perceptions, but only if I substitute some perception (say the word "triangle") for the triangles I see displayed do I actually signify the triangular forms displayed. It does not follow that there is one triangular form somehow behind these instances. The triangles displayed need only be similar to one another (incompatible in many ways, but still possessing three sides).

Or I may notice that thunder and lightning stand in a certain relation to one another, and I may substitute some perception (say the word "succession") for that relation. I signify succession in this case by substituting the word for certain forms displayed by thunder and lightning taken together as parts of a single, larger perception of which thunder and lightning are both parts. And the same goes for any comparison of forms I may notice. I may notice that perception X is bigger (or smaller, or prettier, or uglier, etc.) than perception Y, but only if I substitute some perception (say the word "bigger") for the comparison in question, can I practically signify that comparison.

Any perception is a sign with regard to what it represents, contrasts with, and is related to. Representation is direct signification; contrast and relation of perceptions, and signification of forms and comparisons, are indirect significations. To the degree to which a perception is represented, it is actually reproduced (ideally, to the point of

Signs 91

identity), so that what is significant is presented through its signification. With contingency and relation, however, what is significant is not so presented. Here signification succeeds only insofar as the sign and the signified (both perceptions) are both parts in a larger perception—one which the signifying part also recalls. Thus contrast and relation, as vehicles of signification, rely on a part recalling the whole, something that can occur only insofar as we already possess either the whole itself, or a representation of it.

As far as signifying forms, and the comparison of forms, is concerned, the same considerations obtain. Signification here too depends on recall, that is, representation, insofar as it is necessary to represent at least some perception in which those forms are displayed. But insofar as all forms are displayed by a variety of similar if not different perceptions, the perfect or pure display of any form is impossible. Our signification of forms, therefore, is no better than those perceptions we are able to cite in which those forms appear. To signify comparisons of forms we need to represent those larger perceptions, or situations, in which those comparisons—that is, the representing or contrasting perceptions—are parts. Here too it is a matter of recalling those larger perceptions.

*

To sum up: although representation itself directly signifies, by virtue of what it is as representation, it must also support the indirect modes of signification—including most names, and all punctuations and evaluations—which are not themselves representational. Perceptions are the condition of all signification. If a perception cannot represent what it signifies because what it signifies is not a perception, we can still represent the perception in which the signified is displayed (although always at the risk of mistaking the signified for the perception in which it happens to be displayed, or for a name when it is a punctuation or evaluation).

*

Any group of perceptions together used as signs constitute a notation. There are many notations, and most are composed of names

92   The Soul

and punctuations and values. Consider, for example, the following score of the beginning of a Bach fugue:

Allegro

The score itself, as a visual perception, consists of two staffs, each divided by vertical lines into several measures, onto which are imposed a variety of further visual marks. These marks include: the large vertical bracket enclosing both staffs at the left; a treble clef mark above and a bass clef mark below; the word ALLEGRO; the numerals 6 and 8 after each clef; the italicized letters *mf*; and a series of notes, phrase-lines, rests, etc. All of these parts, which combine to display the perception of the score as a whole, stand variously as names, punctuations, and values.

*

To see how the score is a notation, let us begin with those parts of the score that are names. The most prominent of these are the notes which name individual tones, and which, taken together, signify the theme of the fugue:

The pattern of these visible notes constitutes a literal picture of the audible pattern of tones which is the theme of the fugue. But the theme is not all that is represented by the score; there are other names in it as well. Consider this part of the score:

This also constitutes a picture, albeit of a group of tones rather than a musical theme. The lines of the staff, and the spaces above, between, and below are the names of individual tones (A, B, C, etc.), with the horizontal extension of the staff-lines and spaces corresponding to the sustained presence of those tones, while the vertical lines, segmenting the staff into sections or measures, name rhythmic units.

Thus our musical score constitutes a composite picture, a kind of double-exposure. On the one hand, it pictures a specific theme, or melody; on the other hand, it pictures a whole musical system, a structure of harmoniously related tones such as can be struck, say, on the keyboard of a piano. By superimposing these two pictures, the score pictures a musical system, parts of which are highlighted as a foreground (the theme), against the background of the entirety of that system (the staffs). In short, an ordinary musical score pictures not just a melody but also a tonal-rhythmic system from which the melody is to be picked-out, as it were, just as a photograph pictures not just a particular sight but also a visual system through which that sight emerges.

A score fills in only some of the possibilities of what can be heard in a given tonal system, just as a photograph fills in only some of the possibilities of what can be seen in a given visual system. Thus a composition in, say, a major key, constitutes a different musical system from a one in a minor key, just as a black-and-white photograph constitutes a different visual system from a color photograph. Any photograph (black and white, color, filtered, etc.) displays the visual spectrum with which it works, just as it displays certain visual objects through that spectrum—it is in this sense that every photograph is a double exposure. And once we learn to use visual names for musical tones, we can recognize what is represented by the score in just the same way as we can recognize what is represented by a photograph (where, names and perceptions named both being visual, we do not have to learn to see-hear them).

*

Our score also includes parts which are punctuations rather than names, most prominently the treble and bass clef signs, the numerals 6 and 8, and the rest signs. These signify nothing about either the tonal-rhythmic system or the theme. Rather they are substitutions for relations exhibited by the score itself, by the music itself, or by the score and music taken together—or else they are substitutions for the lack of such relations. The first two of these punctuations in our example—the treble and bass clef signs, and the numerals 6 and 8—signify that the measured staffs and theme are to be related to one tonal-rhythmic system rather than another (the one with six beats to the measure with the eighth note getting one beat). The treble-clef sign itself represents nothing musical. It simply stands proxy for the correspondence of the standard five line staff with certain tones rather than others. In the treble-clef system, the tone corresponding to the lowest line on the staff is named E, the tone corresponding to the space between that line and the line above it is named F, and so on. And, of course, the bass-clef sign signifies a corresponding coordination of tones with the accompanying staff.

In the same way, the numerals 6 and 8 represent nothing musical (and, indeed, nothing at all save other instances of those numerals). 6 stands for the correspondence of a six-beat om-pa-pa-om-pa-pa rhythm with the tonal system (in this case, the key of C major). 8 stands for the correspondence of each rhythmic unit with the duration of an eight note, with the other notes (longer and shorter) adjusted accordingly. Finally, the rest signs signify the lack of a relation between the tonal-rhythmic system and any theme that might be inscribed upon it (or upon a part of it). These signs too represent nothing at all save themselves. In our example, the entire bass-staff and the lower part of the treble-staff display rest marks in lieu of any notes at all.

All these punctuations—clef signs, numerals, and rests—function more or less as stage directions. They say, given certain visual perceptions to be used as names for musical tones, that those perceptions should be coordinated with one another and with those tones in one highly specific way. In just the same way, stage directions punctuate the course of a drama by signifying highly specific ways in which, say, the actors should stand toward one another and the audience, etc. Sometimes stage directions can put the actors offstage, or clear the stage entirely, etc. Stage directions are as much a part of a dramatic script as clef-signs, numerals, and the rest, are a part of a musical score. Yet the actors on stage do not read out the stage directions as they read out their lines; nor do musicians somehow articulate clef-signs, rest signs, and so on, as part of their performance. Both simply obey these punctuations: they effect (or refrain from effecting) the relations that are punctuated, and so, what is represented and not represented. Yet these punctuations themselves represent nothing apart from themselves (except incidentally).

*

Finally, our score also includes parts which are values rather than names or punctuations, Most prominent in our example is the word ALLEGRO and the sign *mf*. These signify neither perceptions nor relations among perceptions; they signify comparisons among perceptions. The ALLEGRO sign neither names another perception nor punctuates some relation (or lack thereof) between perceptions. Instead it draws a comparison between the music represented in the score and other pieces of music with regard to the tempo or pace of the rhythm. We have here not a simple black-and-white comparison but a continuum of varying intensity between slow and fast, or LARGO and PRESTO. ALLEGRO lies closer to PRESTO than to LARGO, just as ANDANTE lies closer to LARGO than to PRESTO, and so on.

The *mf* sign draws another comparison, this one between degrees of volume, or loudness, vis-a-vis the score in question and the music it represents, on the one hand, and other pieces of music on the other. Here we have another continuum, this time lying between very loud *ff*, (or fortissimo), and very soft *pp*, (or pianissimo), with *mf*, (or mezzo-forte), somewhat closer to the former than to the latter. The *mf* sign signifies that the Bach fugue stands in a certain dynamic comparison to other pieces of music, that is, that it is to be played just so loud, no more or less so.

These signs of comparison, or values, are also like stage directions. They too are part of the script, as it were. But rather than telling us that we should do this or that (that is, that we should effect, or refrain from effecting, this or that relation among perceptions), they tell us that what we do should have a certain quality or desirability vis-a-vis certain other perceptions. Comparisons mark out qualities, but they do not tell us what to do to achieve those qualities: that is the job of punctuations.

*

A musical score, then, is a notation, a sign system that stands in representation and contrast to other perceptions through various configurations of names. The punctuations of the score integrate these configurations of names (staffs and themes) by marking certain non-picturing relations (and non-relations) between them. This tells us, without ambiguity, which notes name which tones. The values of the score indicate the comparative quality of the music represented by the score with regard to other pieces of music. The matter would end there, were things quite as neat as that. They are not, however, for the same parts of a score may serve more than one purpose: a name might also be a punctuation, and possibly a value as well.

Even a note is hardly a pure name; it is at the same time black or white, with or without a staff, and if with a staff, with or without a flag, or flags, and so on. These other parts of notes are values. They indicate not any relation among notes but the duration each note has vis-a-vis other notes (given, say, a quarter note as a unit). Or, to take another example, the 6/8 time of our score is a value as well as a punctuation insofar as, by virtue of that time, it stands in a comparison with other scores (and the music they represent). Yet in these and many other instances definitiveness of function is not obscured by the superimposition of functions upon one item. That a note is, say, both a name and a value does not make it any the less of either of these. Nor need its being both interfere with its being the one or the other. And so on for other superimpositions of names, punctuations, and values.

*

An even simpler notation than a musical score is an alphabet, for example, the standard English alphabet. The visual parts of the alphabet include the familiar twenty-six letters, from A through Z. And these higher-case letters each have their familiar corresponding lower-case counterparts, from "a" through "z". But further, the alphabetic script includes a number of signs which are not letters, and not usually included as part of the alphabet, namely: " ' ( )—: ; . ? ! / Yet these signs are as much parts of any alphabetic script as, say, numerals such as 6/8 and marks such as *mf* are parts of a musical score. It so happens that what we conventionally call the alphabet are those script signs that function predominately as names, that is, the letters, while the others, which function predominately as punctuations and values, we usually leave out. That we call only letters the alphabet is a result, no doubt, of how we learned to read and write as children. But, properly speaking, we should include these other signs in the alphabet, as does any standard keyboard. Indeed, a computer keyboard is a fuller indication of our actual alphabet. Perhaps, then, after the traditional ABC alphabet song, we should add another stanza:

> *Double-quote, single-quote, left and*
> *right parenthesis,*
> *Dash, colon, semi-colon, comma.*
> *Period, question-mark, and exclamation point!*

That the individual letters of the conventional alphabet stand as names for certain spoken sounds is obvious enough. Of course, while some letters stand for certain sounds and only those sounds, others correspond with a number of often quite different sounds. According to the "Key to Pronunciation" of *The Shorter Oxford English Dictionary*, the letters b, d, f, k, l, m, p, t, v, and z each correspond to a single distinct sound, or phoneme, while the rest of the letters correspond to two or more phonemes. Yet the choices are narrow enough, and the combinations of letters (and phonemes) consistent enough, so that, given the conventions of usage, there is little practical difficulty in determining in almost every case which phoneme is indicated by which letter.

The result is that combinations of letters function effectively to display the forms displayed by the combinations of the phonemes they name. As a visual perception, a letter stands in consistent contrast to the perception(s) it names, that is, to its corresponding phoneme(s). But combinations of such letters stand in consistent representation as pictures of those perceptions constituted by the phonemes named by those letters, when those phonemes are ordered in the same way.

Thus the visual combination of letters PHILOSOPHY pictures a certain audible combination of phonemes, and so on.

We do not normally consider an alphabet a picturing medium since it does not obviously picture anything visual (except other visual instances of itself), yet an alphabet succeeds precisely because it is, among other things, a picturing medium, though what it pictures is audible rather than visual. Just as we can see only if we once learned to see, hear only if we once learned to hear, and so forth, so we can see-hear only if we once learned to see-hear. And indeed, we learned to read scripts and musical scores and other notations by learning to see-hear in certain specific ways. Our writing teacher taught us by pointing to the visual letters in the book or on the blackboard while having us utter the corresponding phonemes—when there was more than one corresponding phoneme we practised them separately. And our music teacher taught us by pointing to the lines and spaces on the staff while striking the corresponding keys on the piano; and so on for other notations.

Of course, we cannot picture how it is that a visual script pictures audible speech; this is something we must learn to appreciate, that is, to see-hear primitively for ourselves. But, once we have learned to see-hear, we are in a position to speak out the string of phonemes corresponding to any letters we see (and vice-versa). Thus, in learning scripts and scores, we learn a series of visual-audible perceptions. And since we also learn to coordinate each of these perceptions with specific thoughts, we actually learn, in each case, a tripartite visual-audible-mental perception. And someone who has not learned to read a script, or a musical score, will not be able to speak or think the audible and mental perceptions corresponding to the names in the script or score. They will flunk any test which requires them to do so. They will be unable to recognize the script or score as a picturing medium in the sense discussed above.

*

The punctuations that appear in ordinary English alphabetic script name no sounds; nor do they represent any forms displayed by sounds. Rather the punctuations signify certain uses to which we customarily put various stretches of script (or speech). They literally punctuate—that is, point out—such uses. These are invariably relations into which letters and corresponding phonemes enter (or fail to enter).

For example, a period . signifies the lack of a certain relation between the groups of letters preceeding it and those following it. The letters preceding a period are related to one another in certain ways, and the period merely marks the self-contained integrity, the internal relations, of those letters. In this way, a period is a limit or negation, as is any space between letters. Spaces between letters signify the limits of groups of internally related letters (ordinarily called words). Periods mark off more or less larger independent patterns of letters (sentences). Paragraphs mark off still larger groups; and so on. What is punctuated with regard to each of these groups is the lack of any further relation by some further part to the parts already related together.

Some of the other common punctuations of the alphabet are variations of the period, namely: the coma, the colon, and the semi-colon. Each in its own way is a weaker version of the period. At least one other group of alphabetic punctuations should be noted, namely quotations marks or parenthetical brackets. These function somewhat like the clef-signs in music. Their role is to mark the proper relation between scripts being superimposed on one another. Quotation marks signify that an independent piece of discourse is being brought into relation with the discourse at hand. Parenthetical brackets signify that a dependent piece of discourse is being brought into relation with the discourse at hand.

Finally, the values that appear in ordinary English alphabetic script neither name sounds, nor represent forms displayed by sounds, nor signify relations. Rather they signify certain qualitative comparisons vis-a-vis the script on the one hand, and speech and perceptions beyond speech on the other. The more obvious values include the exclamation point and the question mark. The use of upper-case letters for emphasis is another. If I write THE TRUTH SHALL MAKE YOU FREE I introduce a comparative distinction for these words that sets them off against the ordinary script around them, in which they might also be stated, although with less emphasis.

Let us consider one further example of a notation, and perhaps one of the simplest: the system of natural or whole numbers. The visual parts of the number system—the numerals—are these: 0 1 2 3 4 5 6 7 8 9. In addition, these numerals are often accompanied in numerical script by the following signs, + - = x [ ] < > ÷ among others. The numerals are names, but what it is they name is not as apparent as it is in the case of notes or letters. For the latter are correlated with certain specific perceptions (tones and phonemes), while numerals correspond—or so it seems—with an almost indiscriminate variety of perceptions. If the numeral 5, for example, names certain perceptions (as does the letter b or the note middle C), they are much more various and dispersed (than those named by the letter b and the note middle C). Indeed, they are so much more various and dispersed as to lack any common integrity.

However, this seems mysterious only insofar as we take names to be proper names. Numerals are certainly not (at least not normally) proper names. But all names need not be proper names; there are names that function more widely and flexibly—more like pronouns than proper names—and it is in this way that numerals are used. Just as "he," "she," and "it," are very widely and indiscriminately used in ordinary language to name a great many, sometimes incompatible perceptions, so are 1, 2, 3, etc., used in the same way. The numerals 1 through 9 actually stand as names in the following way: 1 is consistently correlated with any perception simply on the grounds that it is a perception; 2 is consistently correlated with that perception and another that more or less represents it; 3 is consistently correlated with these perceptions and still another that more or less represents them; and so on. We can continue in this way indefinitely, as long as there are similar things to count (they need only be similar enough to one another to constitute a foreground distinguishing them from other things constituting a background). The things we ask children to count—fingers, sheep, coins, pencils, flower petals, etc.—are after all quite similar to one another, and generally presented against a dissimilar background. In other words, some degree of representation is required of perceptions if we are to use numerals to name them. Or, to put it in extreme terms, contingent perceptions can be distinguished, but not counted, and identical perceptions can be counted, but not distinguished.

Although we can count an indefinite number of similar perceptions, the number system is not a simple linear projection. 10 is not simply the next number after 9, standing in the same relation to 9 that 9 stands to 8. 10 is rather the number 1 reintroduced, this time not as the name of 9 perceptions which represent one another in addition to another that represents them, but of all of these *as a single perception*; that is, 10 is the name of a single perception (any perception) whose 9 plus 1 parts all represent one another. The 0 is introduced to the right of the 1 to show that no more than one such perception is named. 0 is a placeholder, indicating no perception but rather the limits of a perception; 0 is used in this case as a punctuation, not as a name.

My point can be brought out by considering how numerals can be ordered, or set out. The conventional sequence goes like this: 1 2 3 4 5 6 7 8 9 10 11 12 13 and so on. But this reflects the application of numerals in counting, not how it is that they act as names and punctuations. To clarify the latter numbers might better be set out as follows, as on an automobile odometer:

$$000000000$$
$$000000001$$
$$000000002$$
$$000000003$$
$$000000004$$

And so on.

Philosophers of mathematics have focused on the linear progression of what they call numbers (mistaking the counting function of numerals for their naming function), and worried over problems of succession and infinity. But the numerical matrix is circular, not successive. It can be expanded or deepened (by widening or narrowing the rows), but it always closes by turning back into itself. Indeed, any numerical matrix, insofar as it is a matrix, is a closed system. In this way, it is very much like the alphabetical matrix we call alphabetical order, except instead of a ten-place system the alphabet exhibits a twenty six-place system:

```
a a a a a a a a a a a a a a a a a a a a a a a a a a
a a a a a a a a a a a a a a a a a a a a a a a a a b
a a a a a a a a a a a a a a a a a a a a a a a a a c
```

And so on to the following conclusion:

```
z z z z z z z z z z z z z z z z z z z z z z z z z x
z z z z z z z z z z z z z z z z z z z z z z z z z y
z z z z z z z z z z z z z z z z z z z z z z z z z z
a a a a a a a a a a a a a a a a a a a a a a a a a a
a a a a a a a a a a a a a a a a a a a a a a a a a b
```

And so on again.

One difference, of course, is that we have no letter in the alphabet which plays the function which 0 plays in numerical order. The reason for this is that we do not use the alphabet for counting, at least not for counting in the manner in which we count using Arabic numerals. If we were to do so, we would have to introduce a new letter, say /, to function in the manner of 0. And if we did that, we could then exchange numerical and alphabetical notations for one another in virtually any situation.

*

Some passages in Wittgenstein's *Remarks on the Foundation of Mathematics* are instructive with regard to numerical order and counting. In paragraph #37, for instance, he gives a description of how we learn to count:

"Put two apples on a bare table, see that no one comes near them and nothing shakes the table; now put another two apples on the table; now count the apples that are there. You have made an experiment; the result of the counting is probably 4. (We should present the result like this: when, in such-and-such circumstances, one puts first 2 apples and then another 2 on a table, mostly none disappear and none get added.) And analogous experiments can be carried out, with the same result, with all kinds of solid bodies.—This is how our children learn sums; for one makes them put down three beans and then another three beans and then count what is there. If the result at one time were 5, at another 7 (say because, *as we should not say*, one sometimes got added, and one sometimes vanished of itself), then the first thing we said would be that beans were no good for teaching sums. But if the same thing happened with sticks, fingers, lines and most other things, that would be the end of all sums."

In paragraph #36, Wittgenstein gives an account of how we extend our counting by compounding it, or doubling it up:

"Imagine you have a row of marbles, and you number them with Arabic numerals, which run from 1 to 100; then you make a big gap after every 10, and in each 10 a rather small gap in the middle with 5 on either side: this makes the 10 stand out clearly as 10; now you take the sets of 10 and put them one below another, and in the middle of the column you make a bigger gap, so that you have five rows above and five below; and now you number the rows from 1 to 10.—We have, so to speak, done drill with the marbles."

What Wittgenstien calls doing drill with the marbles can be read as an account of how we use numbers as names in conjunction with the punctuation 0. His illustration shows how we reintroduce the same numerals as names not of individual marbles but of what he calls sets or rows of marbles. These sets are not logical abstractions (not abstract classes or sets or logical functions, etc.) but *actual rows of marbles*. The reuse of names, distinguished by the appropriate addition of 0s, is what allows us to compound or double up the counting process. In the Arabic number system, counting beyond 9 is a matter of *compounding* numbers, not adding them. A 0 after a 1, as we have seen, names one perception of 9 similar perceptions plus one more similar to them; the compound number 11 names 1 perception as just described (that is, a compounded perception) plus yet 1 more part, similar to the parts of the compounded perception; and so on for 12, 13, and the rest. And the entire process is compounded over again once we have 9 of these compounded perceptions plus one more similar to them: that gives us 100. And so on for 1000, 10,000, 100,000, etc.

Again, the 0 punctuation names no perception, but marks off certain relations in which countable perceptions stand to one another. A 0 marks the relations which obtain between what we normally call "ten" perceptions—these perceptions being more or less similar to one another, and more or less different from their common background (as in Wittgenstein's example). The addition of another 0—going from 10 to 100—merely marks out another "ten," only here we have ten groups of tens; and so on. If similar perceptions are not related to one another, they do not constitute a larger perception, and cannot be counted.

*

0s are the punctuations, or placeholders, of counting, although we also use them, in another way, to indicate the absence of something or anything countable; that is, we use them in various situations to mark the lack of a counting relation. And, of course, there are other numerical relations besides counting, and they have their appropriate punctuations. For example, we add, subtract, multiply, and divide numerals. All of these, insofar as they involve more than single digits, presuppose our ability to count. Addition is the simple conjunction of countable perceptions into a larger perception; subtraction is the simple disjunction of countable perceptions into smaller perceptions; multiplication and division are systematically further-compounded versions of addition and subtraction, respectively. The signs for these operations, + - x and ÷, are the punctuations that tell us to relate (or unrelate) various numerals.

A number of other numerical signs, however, are values rather than names or punctuations. The sign of equality = marks a comparative evaluation of numerals, or groups of numerals, as does the sign of inequality ≠. In the numerical statement 7 + 5 = 12, the = is not a mark of relation; it does not tell us to bring the 12 into any relation to the 7 + 5 (although the + of the 7 + 5 does tell us to bring the 7 and the 5 into relation with one another). Instead, the = signifies that when 7 is added to 5 the result will be the same as 12. Other numerical values, for example < and >, function in the same way. Insofar as ambiguity of function is concerned, it is found less in the numerical system than in other common notations. To a considerable extent, the names,

Signs

punctuations, and values we use in arithmetic play only their respective roles as names, punctuations, and values.

*

Let me be more precise about names, punctuations, and values. If a name contrasts with the perception it names, then we have a label; if a name represents the perception it names, then we have a reproduction. (The names of the notations in the examples above are labels.) But representation and contrast are not themselves naming, for naming requires a relation between names and perceptions named, as well as the ability to substitute the name for the perception named. The relationship between name and perception named need not be established every time we use a name, but it must be available (that is, at least representable) upon demand. To establish a perception as a name, that is, to relate it to what it names, is to find its place as a part, along with the perception it names, in a larger perception. Our ability to produce, or at least represent that larger perception, is the means by which we can reestablish that name as a name when asked to do so.

But for a perception to function as a name it must also be substituted for the perception it names. Lightning is related to thunder more or less as names are related to what they name, and lightning stands as a name for thunder by virtue of that very relationship. And this is so even though we cannot literally produce lightning whenever we want to signify thunder. Of course, we also call lightning a sign of thunder because of further perceptions which we can substitute for one another (thought and words) which are themselves the names for thunder and lightning.

The great advantage of names such as visual marks and audible sounds, once they are established, is that we can easily combine and recombine them with one another. As convenient visual marks, or spoken sounds, or thoughts, names can be shuffled with relative ease, in comparison with most of the sensible perceptions they name. These latter, insofar as they are dispersed through the physical universe, can often be combined only with the greatest physical effort, and often not at all. By combining names, then, we can represent combinations of the perceptions they name—whether these are thoughts or sensations. If I write CAT, I am putting down a combination of letters that represents either a combination of phonemes, or a combination of tactions (as in Braille), or a combination of thoughts. In this case, where the names or letters stand more or less in contrast to the perceptions they name, the resulting representation is either a picture or an analog.

In other words, CAT represents a complex sound, and/or taction, and/or thought. But it does so only insofar as I have linked up C and A and T and the rest of the alphabet with certain sounds, tactions, and thoughts, and insofar as that linkage is itself representationally sustained for me. In other words, if I am asked how it is that CAT stands as an alphabetic representation, all I can do is represent how it is that the alphabet is taught and learned: the teacher at the blackboard, writing letters, sounding phonemes, pointing to the one while speaking the others, and so on. In short, I cannot represent naming as such, for naming is not a perception but a relation. But since I can represent the larger perception, or situation, in which a name and the perception named are themselves related, I can display the naming relation. That is, I can display an instance of naming, and another, etc., but nothing that might construe naming as a perception.

Punctuations and values, unlike names, stand neither as representations and contrasts, nor as relations, to what they signify. For perceptions cannot stand in these ways to forms, nor to the comparison of forms, but only to other perceptions. Yet relations and comparisons cannot be signified apart from their realization in and through perceptions. Unless we can also signify the perception which displays the forms and comparisons that concern us, we cannot signify those forms and comparisons at all. Therefore, punctuations and values accompany names, or, as in a notation, a series of names representing a perception. And as we have seen, they are themselves parts of scores, scripts, and numerical notations. But we cannot represent punctuation and evaluation as such, no more than we can represent naming as such. What we can represent are instances of punctuation and evaluation, just as we can represent instances of naming.

But there is a distinction here. An instance of naming, through showing us a perception that is named, shows us both what the name signifies and the naming relation. It does this by putting the name as a perception and the perception named together in a larger perception. But an instance of punctuation or evaluation, though showing us a perception that is punctuated or evaluated, cannot show us any punctuating or evaluating relation. We can relate our punctuations and evaluations (as the perceptions that they themselves are) to the perceptions whose forms and comparisons we seek to punctuate and evaluate, thus constituting a larger perception we can represent. But this still fails to represent punctuation or evaluation, or even what is punctuated or evaluated, even though a series of such representations will distill the forms and comparisons in question.

Punctuation and evaluation are rooted in distinguishing the same or similar forms and comparisons in different perceptions. We track the forms and comparisons that concern us through a great variety, if need be, of differing perceptions. By representing this process, the forms and comparisons are isolated and approximated in the only way possible. Someone who punctuates or evaluates properly is able to follow a rule to apply a principle in a variety of situations. But the only evidence or demonstration we can have of this is a description or representation of his or her doing so. So even punctuation and evaluation can be resolved into representational terms, albeit indirectly.

CHAPTER SIX

Language

Any language—say, English—is a notation no different in essentials from an alphabetic script, a musical score, a number system, or any other kind of notation. Certain combinations of phonemes (or letters) usually serve in any language as names, punctuations, and values, although individual phonemes (or letters) sometimes serve this way as well. These individual signs and their combinations we call words. More precisely, a word (whatever kind of sign it may be) is any phoneme or cluster of phonemes that recurs in speech independently but in combination with other such words (or any letter or cluster or letters that does the same in script). In grammatical terms, a word can be virtually anything: an article, a prefix, a suffix, a root, a noun, a verb, a gerund, a phrase, a cliche, an adjective, an adverb, and so on. But grammatical parts of speech are beside the point here. For words are those parts of language that can be distinguished as names, punctuations, and values, and not as parts of speech.

Words, insofar as they are names, stand in relation to other words so as to constitute sentences, which, insofar as they are so constituted, represent or contrast with those perceptions whose parts are named by those words. In other words, sentences, insofar as they are composed of names, are perceptions which represent or contrast with other perceptions. And insofar as words are punctuations, they stand in relation to other words in sentences, not as the constituents of any representation or contrast, but as significations of various relations.

And finally, insofar as words are values, they also stand in relation to other words in sentences, although neither as the constituents of any representation or contrast, nor as significations of various relations, but because they signify comparisons.

Consider the following sentences:

>give me money
>run home
>i love you
>shoot him dead
>nine men play ball

Each of the familiar terms in these sentences is most easily construed as a name. That is, each term corresponds for the community of English speakers to certain more or less specific perceptions. Thus in "give me money" the term "give" corresponds to a certain gesture (surrendering something or someone); "me" corresponds to everybody's own self; and "money" corresponds to legitimate currency, or acceptable substitutes thereof, however defined ("legal tender for all debts public and private"); and so on.

Names are established and maintained through more or less consistent usage. When a few names are put together, such as "give me money," the question is whether the perception which they constitute represents anything other than itself or its alphabetic counterpart (in this case, the audible version of "give me money"). Whether or not, or to what extent it does so, is clear to any speaker of the language, that is, to anyone who has learned what the names name. The visual combination "give me money" is indeed representative of more than the corresponding audible words since the non-linguistic perceptions named by each term actually can and do coincide with one another to produce a larger non-linguistic perception, or a whole family of such perceptions: namely, those in which I (or anyone else) am given money. Insofar as most names contrast with the perceptions they name, the collective representations they constitute are mostly pictures or analogies, although onomatopoeic names suggest stronger representations, even identities.

On the other hand, combinations of names can fail to represent anything other than themselves and their alphabetic counterparts. But in language this occurs only when we have failed to learn what the names of the language name, or indeed, what any of the signs signify. If I hear spoken a language entirely foreign to me—say, Mandarin Chinese—I hear a series of sounds. If I attend carefully to those sounds over time, I should be able to isolate recurring sounds, recurring patterns, and so on. I could even work out the syntactical rules of the language, perhaps even to the point where I could detect syntactical errors made by the speakers. I might even reach the point where I could anticipate certain responses, so that if the first speaker said X, I could correctly anticipate that the second speaker should say Y. But even with all of this, I would not know what the language was about, that is, what, other than the language itself, was being signified. But if I learn what the signs of the language signify, and especially what the names name, then there can hardly be any combination of names in that language that can fail to represent something to me.

For example, even phrases such as "seven you butter" or "me wood pickle" or "round square" have some representational capacity, if for no other reason than that almost any combination of names (if I know what each name names) can be reproduced at least as a combination of thoughts, given our ability to freely substitute thoughts for one another. In other words, even if I can find no combination of sensations corresponding to a given combination of names, I can almost always produce one in thought so as to give that combination of names something to represent. The poet writes "burnt out ends of smoky days," and somehow that finds a referent, at least in my thoughts. Even "seven you butter" and "me wood pickle" somehow find referents, at least in thought. After all, "seven you butter" suggests: you butter seven (pieces of toast?); and "me wood pickle" suggests: I am going to pickle some wood (something which might, under some circumstances, be a plausible thing to do); and "round square" suggest: well, a round square, perhaps as follows —

Some would object that "round square" is a self-contradictory phrase, but that begs the issue posed by the very existence of the phrase itself (not to mention the drawing above). It is true that a circle is not a square, and a square not a circle, but we should hardly expect a "round square" to be one or the other; rather we should expect it to be somehow both at once, as the figure above seems to be.

To say that a sentence or proposition or phrase is self-contradictory is to say that it is false (does not obtain, cannot be represented) in any possible world (in any possible thought or sensation). But it is by no means clear that there is no possible world in which any given conjunction of referents named cannot occur, at least not as long as we can substitute any thought for any other. There is at least a thought-world, for example, in which the United States both did and did not enter World War I in 1917, say one in which the United States did not declare war but sent troops covertly; or, if we like, one in which there are two United States, one which entered the war and one which did not; and so on. The burden of proof seems to lie with those who insist that there are self-contradictions of this sort.

Thus, in naming, representation is never entirely particularized, just as, by the same token, it is never entirely universalized. No perception we know can be entirely contingent to everything else, nor can anything be identical to everything else. All perceptions are true (that is, representations of other perceptions) in at least some possible world (that is, in thought if not in sensation), but no perception is true in all possible worlds (that is, in all thoughts and sensations). For only if all perceptions represented one another completely could any (and every) perception be true in all possible worlds. But then, all perceptions would be identical to one another (all would be identical with all), which is manifestly not so.

On the other hand, all perceptions are false (that is, they contrast with other perceptions) in at least some possible world (that is, in some thought or sensation), but no perception we can know is false in all possible worlds (that is, in all thoughts and sensations). If a perception were false in all possible worlds, except that which it constitutes in itself, it would contrast with all other perceptions. It could not be represented at all, so that we could not even know that it was false in all possible worlds. Indeed, we could not even know it at all, insofar as to know is to represent. So, just as there is no perception that can represent the world (that is, all perceptions), so there is no perception we can know that is without at least some representational capacity.

To put it another way, we can take tautologies (combinations of names, each of which names perceptions so much the same as to turn their combination into merger) as identities, and contradictions (combinations of names, each of which names perceptions so different as to deny any combination of them at all) as contingencies. But, when taken in this way (as above), it becomes clear that as far as combinations of names (sentences) go, there can be no such thing as an unconditional identity, or tautology, or an unconditional contingency, or contradiction. This is how names function in any notation, including language. Naming allows no truth, no representation, to be true everywhere, or nowhere. There are no necessarily true or false combinations of names.

*

Language, like any notation, consists in punctuations as well as names (and values). Consider the following combinations of words, where the punctuations are italicized:

> pay*ing* toll
> soldiers run*ning*
> *between* jobs
> red hits jack *now*

Punctuations, like names, are words; that is, independently recurring phonemes or clusters of phonemes (in script, letters) which combine with other such words and which have signification. Now any combination of names is a sentence insofar as such a combination represents something somewhere—at least in one possible world. Punctuations, on the other hand, represent or contrast with nothing, and no combination of punctuations can ever be a sentence. Punctuations signify relations, but they do so only by signifying names which, in sentences, display the relations in question. Punctuations signify relations by being placed in conjunction with names which either help display those relations in conjunction with other names, or which signify perceptions whose parts display those relations.

For example, the "ing" in "paying toll," insofar as it is an independently recurring cluster of letters, remains as distinct a word as any other (even though, given the conventions of alphabetic script, it is not separated from "pay"); and so on for the other punctuations listed above. (Words are not to be equated with those letters or clusters of letters created by the spacing of alphabetic script. Any dictionary recognizes that this is not so by listing independently as words punctuations such as "ed," "s," "ing," and so forth.) *The Shorter Oxford English Dictionary* defines "ing" as "a completed action, a process, habit or act." Clearly, a completed action, process, habit or act is not itself a perception. It is rather a pattern of relations that is displayed by certain perceptions. There are no separate ings to be encountered anywhere, but there is walk-ing, talk-ing, eat-ing, lov-ing, see-ing, think-ing, sleep-ing, and all the other ings. The ing

Language

punctuation added to these terms testifies that the perceptions such terms name display their forms in just that certain active, ongoing manner the dictionary calls a completed action, a process, habit, or act.

The ing punctuation in language is very like the trill punctuation in music: *tr*. And just as there is no tone in music corresponding to the trill-mark itself, so in language there is no perception corresponding to ing. While we can give examples of tones being trilled, we cannot give any example of a trill apart from tones being trilled. And while we can give examples of perceptions inging, so to speak (a man running, a horse feeding, and so on), we cannot give any example of ing apart from specific perceptions which ing.

Since we cannot represent forms themselves (but only the perceptions which display them), we cannot represent what it is that punctuations punctuate. We can distinguish forms from the perceptions which display them insofar as we recognize the same forms displayed by different perceptions, even though we can never distinguish forms from their display by some perception. Thus we recognize a relative but not absolute independence of forms vis-a-vis the perceptions that display them. The question of whether or not forms enjoy an absolute independence from perceptions is a moot point for us since we cannot represent forms apart from perceptions. Thus punctuation depends on naming in a way in which naming does not depend on punctuation, although punctuation is not naming and cannot be reduced to it.

*

Finally, values too are words. Consider the following combinations of words, where the values are italicized:

> *the best* man
> *the greatest* good
> *a beautiful* blue sky
> *hot* water

Values, like names and punctuations, are words, that is, independently recurring phonemes (in script, letters) which combine with other such words, and which have signification. Like punctuations, values represent and contrast with nothing, and no combination of values can be a sentence. Values signify comparisons, but they do so only by signifying names to be compared. As with punctuations, values do their work by being placed in conjunction with names to be compared.

For example, the so-called definite and indefinite articles, "the," "a," and "an," as well as what logicians call quantificational terms, "any," "all," "some," and "one," are all values, as in "*the* best man." All these terms indicate comparisons. We can have either all of a number of things, or some of them, or any of them, or any one of them, or one specific one of them. Each of these choices implies the others. Thus "the best man" is one specific best man of all the best men, whereas we might instead have "all the best men," or "some of the best men," or "a best man," etc. As far as "best" is concerned in this example, it evaluates the name "man" and the perception "man" names, vis-a-vis other appropriate evaluations—most obviously, "worst," "mediocre," etc. And so on for other evaluations.

*

In sum, naming, punctuation, and evaluation function as simply and as distinctly in language as in any other notation. Yet, unlike the relatively simple notations considered in the last chapter, names, punctuations, and values are endlessly superimposed and compounded in language. A name is no less a name in language, but the sign we use as a name may also be used in the language as a punctuation or value, or even both, or all three. Punctuation signs as well may be names and/or values, and value signs may be names and/or punctuations. The point is not to establish which of these a word ought to be, but whether, given some use of that word, it signifies in one, or two, or all three of these ways.

More often than not, one signification predominates in any use of a word. But it frequently does not. After all, any conjunction of names in itself implies a comparison and/or a relation between the perceptions named; and any comparison implies the naming of perceptions and/or their relation; and any relation implies the naming of perceptions and/or their comparison. Thus "lowest" seems to be primarily a punctuation, but its evaluative overtones are obvious ("the lowest scum of the earth"). "Boy" is clearly a name, but a phrase such as "oh boy" has comparative if not punctuating force, while "boys" may be taken as a simple name or as a name and a punctuation; further, "boys," "man," and "men" are names, yet they do the work of singular-plural comparison; and so on ad infinitum.

What we bring to any segment of language is the expectation that it signifies perceptions, relations among perceptions, and comparisons among perceptions. We are interested in what combinations of names represent or fail to represent, and in the ways in which names (and/or their combinations) are punctuated and/or evaluated. To punctuate relations (that is, forms) is to signify just those relations, no matter what perceptions may display them. Punctuation disregards the perceptions that display the relations in question. It is concerned only with their external relations (or, to put it another way, it treats all relations as external relations). To evaluate perceptions, on the other hand, is to compare the forms they display as perceptions. It is to take up relations as internal relations. Comparison is possible only in consideration of what is displayed by one perception and another. To consider relations in disregard of the perceptions that display them is to forgo any basis of comparison. We cannot compare relations qua relations. We can only compare perceptions that display relations.

*

A sustained example will show how names, punctuations, and values function in language. Consider the following passage, which opens Kafka's novel, *The Castle*, as a standard sample of ordinary language:

"It was late in the evening when K. arrived. The village was deep in snow. The Castle hill was hidden, veiled in mist and darkness, nor was there even a glimmer of light to show that a castle was there. On the wooden bridge leading from the main road to the village, K. stood for a long time gazing into the illusory emptiness above him."

If we examine this passage in terms of names, punctuations, and values (that is, if we pick out the primary signification of each word, and the secondary and tertiary ones as they intrude), we get something like the following (items parenthetically enclosed indicate the secondary and tertiary significations):

```
NAMES:         (It)                          eve
PUNCTUATIONS:  It       was    late    in    (eve-ning)   when
VALUES         (It)            (late)        the

NAMES:         K.   arriv          village              snow
PUNCTUATIONS:       (arriv- ed)            was      in
VALUES:             (arriv)        The              deep

NAMES:              (Castle) hill                              mist
PUNCTUATIONS:                    was    den          ed    in
VALUES:        The   Castle          hid-      veil

NAMES:              dark  ness              there        glimmer
PUNCTUATIONS:  and                  nor was       (there)
VALUES:             (dark-ness)                 even a

NAMES:              light            castle       there
PUNCTUATIONS:  of          to     that       was    (there)        On
VALUES:             (light)     show    a

NAMES:              bridge (lead)                    road
PUNCTUATIONS:              lead - ing    from                  to
VALUES:             the         (lead)          the   main

NAMES:              village    K. stood             time   gaz-
PUNCTUATIONS:                        for         (time)      ing
VALUES:             the        (stood)    a     long

NAMES:                         empti- ness              him
PUNCTUATIONS:  into                              above
VALUES:                 the illusory
```

This approach to language should not be misunderstood. It is neither a formal analysis nor an interpretative synthesis. It is neither a reduction of the passage purporting to make plain some underlying struc-

Language 119

ture, nor is it an amplification purporting to bring out some hidden significance. (Those are, respectively, the behaviorist and solipsist approaches to language.) Insofar as Kafka's passage has any underlying structure, it is constituted by the recurring syntactical patterns it displays in common with other passages of standard English; and insofar as the passage has any hidden significance, it is established by symbolic identification of key terms in the passage with other perceptions that interest us. But these are not my concern here. Putting them aside, I am concerned instead to look at just what is represented, and how it is punctuated and evaluated.

Consider the first sentence of the passage: "It was late in the evening when K. arrived." The very first word, "It," stands mainly as a punctuation, and secondarily as both a name and a value. "It" is primarily the answer to the question: When did K. arrive? In this first sentence, "It" signifies "when," which is itself a punctuation of temporal relations; that is, "It" punctuates as a substitute for "when." And in answer to "when" we are told that K.'s arrival "was late in the evening." The punctuation "was" tells us that, as we read, the temporal relation has already been established, while "late," "in," and "evening," add further punctuational refinements: "late" punctuates K.'s arrival to be towards the end of some temporal sequence; "in" punctuates the temporal sequence involved; and "evening" punctuates that sequence itself as a phase among other such sequences (afternoon, night, etc.).

Of course, "late" and "evening," like "It," signify more than relations (whereas, at least in this sentence, "was," "in," and "when" do not). The term "late" also has an evaluative signification: even as it helps to punctuate evening temporally, it also suggests a comparison between that evening (a late evening) and other evenings, which in turn brings out certain characteristics typical of late evenings (darkness, silence, a touch of mystery, etc.), but not of early or mid-evenings. Yet, with all this, "late's" major function in the sentence remains to clarify the temporal relation in question. As far as "evening" goes, I take its primary function to be to name a perception (namely, that specific evening in question). The value "the" tells me it is one specific evening that is in question. Yet the punctuating function of "evening" is nearly as strong as its naming function. It finally establishes the temporal relation between K.'s arrival and where it is that he arrives, that is, at the village (as learned only in the next sentence).

To continue, "K." is such a bare name that it carries no punctuating or evaluative functions. But "arriv" bears all the signifying functions: it names a perception (the event of K.'s arrival); it punctuates a relation (this time, a spatial as well as a temporal one, for K. arrives not only late in the evening but at the village); and it has some evaluative force as well (for certain comparisons are immediately posed, most obviously departure, evoking certain characteristics such as novelty, anticipation, etc.). And "ed" and "." function straightforwardly as punctuations (temporal and grammatical), with no other noticeable function. Finally, to return to "It," we find its naming function tied in to its ability to be substituted for "evening," and its evaluative function tied in to its ability to be substituted for "late."

This account of Kafka's first sentence shows, as a first approximation, how representation, relations, and comparisons are signified in a typical prose passage. However, some refinements should be noted. First, many words, for example, "It" in the first sentence, are substitutions for other words or phrases, and often signify only through the words and phrases for which they are substituted. These substitutions are generally abbreviations, and we learn them as we learn all words. Properly speaking, they are names, but to the extent to which they name only other words or phrases, it is the signifying function of these other words or phrases that placeholders like "It" pick up.

Second, the linear all-in-one-dimension presentation of language, either as a stream of phonemes or as a stream of letters, is profoundly misleading. Language is three-dimensional in signification, and that becomes plain only in a three-level notation such as the one used above. Seen in this way, language looks more like a musical score, but whereas the punctuations and values manifest in a score are generally repressed in a musical performance, they are usually very much part of any linguistic performance. Music is fully notated, but it is not itself a notation. It is a family of audible perceptions exploited for the sake of the forms they display. Language is sometimes used in this way, (as, for instance, in a work like *Finnegans Wake*), but usually it is used as a notation. I shall leave out the "musical" considerations of language (rhyme, rhythm, verse, etc.) only because these are concerned with notation only indirectly. (Of course, it is a mistake to compartmentalize all these functions too severely; the musicality of language, or its lack, is a constant factor conditioning its use and impact, along with its notational dimensions.)

Thirdly, as my account of Kafka's sentence should make clear, we use names, punctuations, and values with a certain flexibility. Kafka's sentence allows of more than one emphasis. For instance, I charted "late" as primarily a punctuation and secondarily as a value, but someone might insist that it also has the overtones of a name, for we sometimes do use "late" as a name. But I think its use as a name is rare to the point of almost never occurring, although it conjures those names with which it is closely associated as a punctuation and value. I also charted "evening" as primarily a name and secondarily as a punctuation, but someone might insist on reversing these priorities, or perhaps even on adding an evaluative dimension to the word as used here. To be sure, "evening" does raise the comparison of "morning," and indeed of all the times of day. But if that evaluative dimension is present, it seems to me to be so only in a tertiary way; and if I place the naming function of "evening" over its punctuating function, it is because the evaluation "the" tells me that some distinct, definite evening, some perception, is in question. But such decisions are always subject to closer reading and further example. And indeed it is not uncommon to be able to read a text in more than one way. The point is that any reading, if I am right, must follow the criteria of naming, punctuation, and evaluation.

*

Language is fundamentally descriptive, although modified by punctuations and evaluations. It is our descriptions (or their lack) that we punctuate and evaluate. Relations and comparisons have no independent existence apart from what is related and compared, that is, apart from perceptions, even though the same relations and comparisons can obtain through a wide variety of perceptions. The sense of language lies in what it represents; that is, insofar as any sample of language succeeds in representing any perception other than itself, it has some kind of sense. Taken in this way, sense (which I use synonymously with meaning) is equivalent to representation (and the lack of sense, or nonsense, to contrast), so that all representation, linguistic and non-linguistic, makes sense. What distinguishes language is not that it makes sense, but that it does so in an economical and convenient manner, and that it combines that with the other features of a notation: punctuation and evaluation.

The test of language is the test of representation. There must be representation, or sense, for there to be communication, and even though it be modified by punctuation and evaluation, some sense must be present in order for any modification to take place. Naming is at the core of the representational view of language. Once we have established names, we can proceed freely to combine and recombine them as we see fit. That is, we can then do with our bodies (tongues, hands, eyes, etc.) and simple materials (pencils, pens, paper, keyboards, chalk, blackboards, etc.) what otherwise we can do only in our thoughts, namely, freely substitute perceptions for one another.

Since the perceptions we can substitute for one another in language are sensations (sounds of speech, marks on paper, etc.), we can duplicate publicly the free activities of otherwise private thoughts. We can think out loud, and we can hear and see others doing so. The names we combine in language constitute perceptions. They in turn represent perceptions constituted by the same or similar combinations of further perceptions which correspond to the names in question. And we can almost always (perhaps always) constitute such a perception—at least in thought. But, again, punctuations and values name no perceptions, literally name no-thing; the relations and comparisons they signify are entirely ineffable, although they are displayed by and through what is not ineffable.

*

It is solipsism and behaviorism which distort the perceptual basis of language. Solipsism, as we have seen, takes similarities (even contingencies) for identities. And in language, the taking of similarities or contingencies for identities, as far as names go, is metaphor. If we say "burnt out ends of smoky days," or "round square," or "man is a wolf," or "the child is father of the man," or "too hot the eye of heaven shines," or "drunk with sight of power," or "the seducer of the people," we produce metaphors. A metaphor says, or presupposes, that X is Y even though X and Y are not identical. But that we can effect such identification in thought, if not sensation, allows it a place in the world of perceptions. In other words, there is at least a mental perception in which smoky days have burnt out ends, and squares are round, and men are wolves, and the child is father of the man, and heaven has an eye, and the sight of power makes us drunk, and the people can be seduced. These are the perceptions which compel the solipsist, and which he makes the criteria for other perceptions. And the free substitution of thought, permitting any possible combination, is what makes this possible.

If our solipsistic tendency in thought is to combine perceptions into identities, our behavioristic tendency in sensation is to separate them as contingencies. And just as in language metaphor is the product of the former, so in language irony is the product of the latter. Irony is the taking of similarities or identities for contingencies. If we say, "the wisdom of God is the folly of this world," or "whom I will trust as I will adders fang'd," or "Hercules, weakest of men," or "peace is war," we produce ironies. An irony says, or presupposes, that X can never be Y even though it seems to be. Indeed, saying that X is Y is precisely what makes it clear to the behaviorist that X is not Y. His criterion is the world of sensation where perceptions are related only in certain ways, and not others.

The behaviorist takes "the wisdom of God" and "the folly of this world" as signifying values displayed through sensations, and by this test he claims that they cannot be the same, since "wisdom" cannot in sensation be "folly"—any more than "trust" cannot in sensation be a matter of "adders fang'd." Indeed, these comparisons, and the identities they presuppose, are literally false in the sensible world (even though they might be represented there, for example, in language). And since the sensible world is the behaviorist's criterion, their equation in thought cannot be admitted (or admitted only as nonsense).

What is curious here is that metaphor and irony cannot be distinguished linguistically. Is "round square" metaphor or irony? Or "peace is war?" Or any of the others? Linguistically, they are all representations of thoughts, not sensations. But we judge them as metaphors or ironies depending upon whether our commitments are solipsistic or behavioristic. No metaphor can survive ironic scrutiny; the behaviorist finally ignores all metaphors. And no irony can be exempt from metaphoric enthrallment; the solipsist finally ignores every irony.

The solipsist, in taking sensations for thoughts, presumes the free substitution of perceptions for one another. His interest is not in what external relations might or might not obtain among the perceptions in question, but in how these perceptions might be resolved into identities, that is, into the same internal relations. This is not to say that the solipsist strives to make all perceptions identical. But he does strive for a system whereby any perception can be identified with an appropriate archetype. One example of this is the capacity of Biblical imagery to absorb (by imputing to it some archetypal identity) virtually any perception. No matter what mundane act I engage in (say, eating lunch), there stands in the Bible some archetypal precedent (perhaps the breaking of bread) which can absorb and mythologize what I do. And, of course, any extended myth has this capacity.

The behaviorist, on the other hand, takes thoughts for sensations and presumes that some relational order (rather than any, or none) is privileged among perceptions. His interest is not in how various perceptions might be resolved into identities, but by what external relations the perceptions in question are (or are not) constrained. His presumption, derived from sensation, is that only some relations, not all, are possible. We might project all kinds of fantasies ("burnt out ends of smoky days," etc.) but only what has been instantiated in sensation according to the laws of science is real to the behaviorist. In his view, we cannot modulate the internal relations of perceptions since these are but the external relations of the parts of those perceptions, and they too must obey the laws of science.

On the perceptual view of language, what the solipsist calls metaphor and the behaviorist irony is a thought which can be expressed in sensation as a picture or analog, but not as any other representation, including identity. Thus "burnt out ends of smoky days" expresses a thought in language as a picture, while a drawing of a centaur expresses a thought in visual graphics as a picture.

The solipsist is correct to insist on the reality and power of metaphor insofar as it remains a possible sensible truth. His error lies in not taking the recalcitrance of the sensible world seriously enough. To treat sensations as thoughts is inevitably to distort them and so to put oneself as their mercy. The behaviorist is correct to insist upon the disenchantment of irony insofar as it deflates the pretensions of thought. His error lies in not taking the power of metaphor seriously enough. To treat thoughts as sensations is to deny their free activity and the products of that activity; it is to be impoverished.

The linguistic consequences of solipsism and behaviorism are considerable. The solipsist reduces punctuation and evaluation to naming. His main preoccupation is with archetypes, and the similar or merely related perceptions conflated with them. Metaphor is the linguistic mode of this identification (and the dead metaphor is the linguistic mode of the stereotypical consolidation of this identification). Myth is no more than extended metaphor.

Even if the solipsist were not enthralled by some archetype, he would still be left with the presumption (derived from thought) of the free substitution of all perceptions. And since the free substitution of perceptions suggests a disregard for how they might or might not be related or compared, the tendency is to ignore punctuations and values, and admit only names as significations. If a punctuation or value cannot be construed as the name of a perception (as in personification, allegory, etc.), it will be nonsensical to the solipsist. There is a simplicity to this solipsistic reduction of signification to naming, but it holds no comfort for those concerned with relations and comparisons of perceptions already named. It is here that solipsism is compromised.

The behaviorist, on the other hand, reduces naming and evaluation to punctuation. Since the conceit of the behaviorist is that thoughts are sensations, and since difference predominates over sameness and similarity among sensations, all perceptions turn out to be contingent to one another. Further, if perceptions are all contingent to one another, each becomes a mystery in itself, a black box or vanishing point beyond comprehension. All that can be done under such circumstances is to mark the external relations of perceptions.

Since external relations turn out to be consistently patterned in some ways rather than others, the behaviorist presumes to sort out such consistent patterning. He becomes preoccupied with isolating and marking the relations among perceptions which obtain (or fail to obtain) consistently. A name in this view becomes not the signification of a perception, but the signification of forms consistently displayed by the external relations of contingent (vanishing) perceptions. And a value in this view becomes not the signification of any comparison of forms, but of a consistent relation between forms to which the behaviorist presumes to reduce their comparison. Names and values, in other words, are construed by the behaviorist as punctuations.

Now the behaviorist is correct to isolate patterned relations wherever he can. Indeed, this is the whole thrust of the scientific enterprise. But the imposition of this presumption on the entire world of perceptions remains a fundamental error of experience. It reduces representation to relation. Representation and contrast, and the comparisons made through them, are not relations, although perceptions display relations. A perception can only be constituted out of the perceptions that are its parts, which must be related together to constitute that perception.

There is nothing implausible or self-refuting, however, about the solipsist's claim that sensations are thoughts, and that similar perceptions (and even perceptions related to similar perceptions) are all identical to one another, since almost always in thought we substitute similar and related perceptions for one another as if they were identical. That we cannot always do so—especially in "sensation"— seems not a fatal objection to the solipsist, but a problem to be overcome in time.

Neither is there anything implausible or self-refuting in the behaviorist's claim that thoughts are sensations, and that similar perceptions (and those related to them) are all different from one another, since this is almost always so in sensation where our ability to substitute perceptions freely is invariably limited. That we can sometimes substitute freely— especially among "thoughts"—seems not a fatal objection to the behaviorist, but a problem to be overcome in time.

*

Behaviorism reduces names and values to punctuations; it presumes that all signification is punctuation. The whole naturalistic, secular view of the world, equated with modernity but already manifest in ancient Greece and Rome, takes behaviorism to heart. It presumes that language is ultimately about forms displayed in nature but separable from it, and captured in thought through science and technology and philosophy. It presumes that language is finally a matter of punctuation, of elaborating a formal system or theory, mathematical or logical.

Solipsism reduces values and punctuations to names; it presumes that all signification is naming. The whole ritualistic, religious view of the world, equated with 'traditional cultures' but manifest as well in 'new age' movements and consumerism and the media, takes solipsism to heart. It presumes that language is ultimately about privileged perceptions, or archetypes, manifest in the natural world as exceptional to it, and demonstrated in sensation through ecstatic visions, miracles, etc. It presumes that language is finally a matter of naming, of designating a concrete mystical vehicle, an epiphany.

Neither solipsism nor behaviorism allows us to speak about the soul. Only the meditative techniques developed by shamans, yogis, Zen masters and others have probed beyond solipsism and behaviorism. For them language was directed beyond thoughts and sensations, beyond perceptions, to what I call the soul. Most have thought it paradoxical, however, to speak of the soul, finding that it can neither be punctuated nor named. I suggest, on the other hand, that the soul linguistically is a value, not a punctuation or name, and that the soul language of value is not paradox but intuition, and that the soul is the most fundamental intuition of all—at least for us. Although value cannot be represented or contrasted or punctuated, it is displayed in the discrepancy of any comparison, with the soul being the greatest discrepancy of any comparison—the discrepancy between perception and non-perception, between unconsciousness and consciousness, between representation and contrast on the one hand, and non-representation and non-contrast on the other.

CHAPTER SEVEN

The Soul

We must speak of persons before we can speak of the soul.

Persons are combinations of physical and mental perceptions. They are perceptions whose parts are thoughts and sensations, but who are themselves neither thoughts nor sensations. Being neither a thought nor a sensation, no person can be part of any thought or sensation. All combinations of physical perceptions are physical perceptions, and all combinations of mental perceptions are mental perceptions. But any combination of physical perceptions (sensations) and mental perceptions (thoughts)—a person—is neither a physical perception nor a mental perception. Call it a super-perception.

As super-perceptions, persons not only have perceptions as parts (sensations and thoughts), but are themselves parts of further perceptions, for example, families, groups, communities, classes, tribes, nations, races, etc. These social perceptions, made up of persons, are also combinations of thoughts and sensations. More accurately, they are combinations of combinations of thoughts and sensations; they are combinations of persons. There is no common term for these combinations of persons. I call them cultures, with the understanding that one can speak of the culture of sex, the culture of glassblowing, the culture of Americans, etc.

The world exists for us as it does because we are persons made up of thoughts and sensations. It is vital to recognize, following Berkeley, that the physical and mental worlds exist through us; we do not exist through them. Persons and the cultural perceptions they constitute are not part of physical nature, or the cosmos; rather the cosmos is part of them. Neither are persons (and cultural perceptions) part of the world of thought; rather the world of thought is part of them. Thoughts and sensations are parts of the super-perceptions we call persons. This is in profound contrast to our solipsistic and behavioristic inclinations, each of which places us as merely parts of the world, whether conceived solipsistically as a private thought world or behavioristically as a public sensation world.

*

A person is only a perception, however, and not yet a soul. Persons without souls—mere combinations of sensations and thoughts—may be possible. Science fiction androids—if they could be given thoughts—would be an example. The soul is not a perception, not even a super-perception. It cannot be perceived in the differentiated part-whole, representation and contrast manner characteristic of perceptions, including persons. A soul is no part-whole differentiation but a distinct if indeterminate consciousness subject to emotion and endowed with a will. Persons are composed of thoughts and sensations, but souls that are persons are aware of the thoughts and sensations that compose them. Consciousness is the hallmark of the soul. Consciousness is the capacity for awareness, not only of perception but of the soul itself. Awareness of the soul by the soul is self-consciousness.

There are at least three aspects of soul of which we have a non-perceptual consciousness. One of these is the will, the independent ability of the soul to act (or not act) in the world of perception. This is a measured freedom, limited by the laws of nature (including the effort of labor) in the world of sensation, but often unlimited in the world of thought. The will is free insofar as it is uninhibited, insofar as it can freely choose to substitute (or not substitute), without hindrance, any perception for any other. Insofar as the will can choose to substitute (or not substitute) any perception for any other, no substitution can be said to be determined by any specific perception.

The second aspect of non-perceptual consciousness is emotion. Emotion is both the reaction of soul to perception and the impact of perception upon the soul. It is a non-part, non-whole self-modification of the soul induced by perception. Emotions, like the will, are not differentiated part-whole phenomena. They are somehow distinct from one another, yet not in terms of any perceptual logic of representation and contrast. And even though distinct, they act pervasively on the soul. The soul is conscious of a spectrum of emotions, including fear, euphoria, desire, belief, melancholy, excitement, boredom, anger, depression, etc. Although emotions are independent of one another, the soul may be conscious simultaneously of more than one emotion, including 'mixed' or contradictory emotions.

The third and ultimate aspect of non-perceptual consciousness is consciousness itself, or awareness. I can do no more than appeal to the reader's intuition of the same. Although we are aware of perceptions, our awareness of perceptions is not something we perceive. Nor is awareness of will and emotion something we perceive. Awareness is the non-perceptual realization that a perception, an emotion, an act of will, or any other intuition is something that I experience but which is other than I am. This amounts to an awareness of awareness—the only awareness we have of ourselves as souls. Awareness—which is what the soul seems to be—is not a thought or a sensation. Nor is it an emotion or an act of will, though these are bridges to and from the soul.

Awareness is the self-conscious capacity for experience, perceptual and otherwise. We are persons because of the specific perceptions—the thoughts and sensations—we have, but we are souls because we are aware of those sensations, and thereby of ourselves. As souls we are not intrinsically persons, or any other set of perceptions. Nor are we our emotions or wills. As souls, we are the capacity for experience, reactive and proactive, perceptual and otherwise. I am extrinsically a body with thoughts, a person leading a life, etc., but I am intrinsically a soul, an awareness, which is not only an awareness of thoughts and sensations, emotion and will, but also an awareness of its own awareness.

My thoughts and sensations constitute an awareness of something other than myself. I sometimes solipsistically confuse my thoughts with myself, and I sometimes behavioristically confuse my sensations with myself. I can also compound my thoughts and sensations and confuse myself with who I am as a person. I do not thereby move beyond thoughts and sensations (or solipsism and behaviorism), but only mis-identify myself with their super-perceptual synthesis, which is my own (or another's) personality. This exaltation of persons—call it humanism or egotism—reinforces rather than overcomes the errors of solipsism and behaviorism. Hence the tragic humanistic vision of an aesthetic-rational humanity capable of beauty and knowledge but inevitably bound to the solipsistic and behavioristic shortcomings of each.

Solipsism, behaviorism, and their combination in humanism are other and alien to myself as a soul, as a consciousness. My soul abides in extra-representational awareness, absorbing perceptions, suffering and enjoying emotions, and acting in turn, when possible, by choosing some experiences over others. For my soul to absorb a perception is to create, however subtly or blatantly, an emotion, a change in the mood of my soul, as it were. The forms of perceptions are somehow de-perceptualized upon their absorption into my soul, where they have their impact as emotions. I (my soul) cannot fail to experience my emotions; I am saturated and sometimes overwhelmed by them. I have learned, with pain, that my emotions can conflict, and in my consciousness of this conflict I have learned to distinguish myself from my emotions. I have also learned that my will is often thwarted or conditioned, and in my consciousness of this frustration I have learned to distinguish myself from my will. We are normally preoccupied with pressing perceptions, powerful emotions, and a sense of free will, and only incidentally are we aware of ourselves as souls. But sometimes (in reflection, meditation, trance-states, altered-states, etc.) we minimize our engagement with perception, emotion, and will so that our self-awareness as souls comes to the fore.

Ordinarily we are conscious of ourselves only as persons, that is, we are conscious only of our perceptual life and its effects in will and emotion. Through these we discover our likes and dislikes, our strengths and weaknesses—all the specific content of perceptual experience which gives us our personalities. This is what is recognizably us: our bodies and their gestures, our thoughts, our habits and desires, our speeches and actions, the times and places we have been, the life-histories we have led, the persons we have known, etc.

The soul, on the other hand, has no such character, no such personality. To us as persons, the soul seems unmediated, and mute: our mysterious, non-perceptual, non-willful, extra-emotional core. The non-perceptual, non-willful, and extra-emotional nature of the soul has led some—Buddhists and others—to the conclusion that souls are literally nothing; that there are no souls. But this conclusion follows only if one makes perceptions the criterion of souls, if one solipsistically or behavioristically confuses perceptions with souls. Of course, the non-perceptual quality of souls, their representational muteness, makes their description impossible, but description is appropriate only to perceptions, not to souls.

Socrates taught long ago that we have no self-knowledge. We do not have the kind of awareness of souls that we have of perceptions, or even of emotions and will. We only "know" the soul negatively as awareness of a non-perceptual evaluative intuition which is also a non-emotion and a non-will. It is impossible to characterize such a thing even metaphorically by references to notions like "distance" and "detachment." Awareness of soul is not a public perception to be shared, or even a private emotion or act of will to be experienced.

*

Let us approach the soul by way of consciousness. As a person I have a specific sort of body and a specific sort of mind. My body is a living, active perception; and my mind, although perhaps not alive in the physical sense, is also an active perception. It is possible, given that bodies and minds are themselves perceptions, that we can have bodies without minds and minds without bodies. The separation of body and mind is not inconceivable. Nor is separation from our waking body-mind inconceivable.

My current consciousness—judging by my earliest memories—originated sometime after the birth of my body, and seems destined to end, or at least be broken, with the death of my body. Indeed, my consciousness is often interrupted, most frequently by sleep, and sometimes by other events (hypnosis, trauma, strong emotions, drugs, virtual reality, etc.). The resulting segments of consciousness are unrelated, except in memory, that is, insofar as they subsequently remember themselves to me, whether perceptually or somehow otherwise.

For the most part my segmented dreams and other non-waking states seem to have less representational carry over, sometimes none at all, in comparison with my segmented waking states. Hence the "reality" we misleadingly credit to waking life. The breaks in my awareness, whether induced by sleep or otherwise, remain mysteries: blanks in my spectrum of representation. The ability to retrieve such discontinuities in life, however, suggests that the discontinuity of death itself may not necessarily be irretrievable. The problem is that it appears that we have to die to find out.

By any practical sense of the word 'separate,' we separate from our bodies and minds when we dream. In dreaming (and in trances, virtual reality, hypnotic states, out-of-body experiences, hallucinations, certain drug-induced states, etc.) our awareness is literally transported to another realm of perceptions. The new stage setting is sometimes similar to that of the waking world, sometimes not, but otherwise unrelated to it. While our souls confront such perceptions, including thoughts and sensations not found in ordinary waking reality, our everyday body-mind continues in repose, asleep or in a trace, or perhaps even carries out activities of its own (e.g., sleepwalking).

If the soul is distinct from its thoughts as well as from its sensations, there is no reason to insist it somehow be connected to certain thoughts any more than to certain sensations. In principle, we can be other persons than the ones we are, perhaps any other person. Such discontinuities of awareness might variously be compounded. It might be possible, for all we know, for two souls (or more) to share one body, to have two bodies at once, or two minds, or both, or more, or less. Nothing we know of perceptions and representation precludes such possibilities, extra-ordinary as they are. In fact, cutting the *corpus collosum*, the tract of nerves connecting the left and right brains, leaves the dominant hemisphere of the brain ignoring the subordinate hemisphere. It is significant (as John C. Eccles points out in *The Human Mystery* and elsewhere) that consciousness apparently follows the dominant hemisphere in such cases, not the subordinate hemisphere; the latter continues to function, but no longer directly for the conscious subject, or soul.

The Soul

Bodies without minds traditionally have been classified as animals, and minds without bodies as spirits. Persons are those perceptions which are at once animals and spirits, and so neither of them. Persons distinguish themselves vis-a-vis animals and spirits precisely through the interplay of sensations and thoughts denied to both the latter. Animals appear to be souls with living bodies, confined to the domain of sensation. They have no thoughts, although they have command of their bodies (and have a will) and appear to have emotions, and therefore probably souls. To have a body without thoughts is to be in an animal world of random-determined sensations, where only the present moment exists, and where to will is to labor. It is to be without the free play of perceptions characteristic of thought.

Spirits, on the other hand, appear to be souls without bodies confined to the domain of thought and emotion. They have no sensations. To be perceptually constituted wholly of thought, to be entirely without sensation, is to be in a world of free-floating mental perceptions. With animals and spirits there is no representation and/or contrast between sensations on the one hand, and thoughts on the other. The issue simply does not arise. Animals have no thoughts to express in sensation; and spirits have no sensations with which to express their thoughts. Animals, if they have souls, are conscious only of sensations, and spirits, if they have souls, are conscious only of thoughts. Other souls may be conscious—for all we know—of yet other perceptions, or non-perceptions.

Had we no thoughts, sensations would still recommend themselves to us, and we would recognize familiar perceptions as a dog recognizes his master, but, like animals, we would remain condemned to the testimony only of those physical perceptions before us at any given time. We would lose the ability to compare what is present with what is absent. Things would remember themselves to us, as it were, only as we encountered them. Animals, armed only with sensations, live in the bosom and on the sufferance of the physical world. For them, behaviorism is sufficient and appropriate. Their sensations are accompanied by no parallel realm of thoughts. Not being able to reflect in thought upon sensation, they cannot represent to themselves sensations that are absent. They are ignorant of antecedents and consequents, of the course of events, of their own fates. They take the world just as it comes.

For spirits, on the other hand, thoughts constitute the entire domain of representation and contrast (which is to say, the entire domain of memory and knowledge). Here there is thought, but no sensation. Forms are recognized only in thought, and nowhere else. Without an ability to display forms outside of thought, there is no escape from thought, nor any need to. For spirits, solipsism is sufficient and appropriate. But not being able to sense means not being able to distinguish sights, sounds, tactions, tastes, and smells; and not to distinguish them is not to distinguish the regularities they embody. The communal public reliability of the physical world vanishes, leaving only the private fluid plasticity of thought.

If animals are condemned to live in the ignorance of the moment, spirits (even with total recall) are isolated from the common world of structured sensation. Not able to publicly reflect in sensation what they privately think, they are unable to find one another according to the guideposts of sensation. If animals are dumb souls trapped in a common world by their sensations, spirits are sleeping souls isolated in their solitary thoughts.

Persons—combinations of sensations and thoughts—combine animality and spirituality. Some of the earliest evidence for persons comes from offerings and other artifacts found in Neanderthal gravesites of about 100,000 years ago. Only a person able to use thoughts to step out of the eternal present of sensation (of animality) could compare the death of a fellow person with the deaths of others (and thus anticipate his or her own death), and to mark this complex realization by some sign. This requires—unlike simple toolmaking or even structure building of which some animals are capable—a mind, that is, a capacity to compare the present with the absent, the moment with what is no longer the moment. But only an ensouled person would mark an event like death—as the Neanderthals did—with contradictory signs of life (gifts, food, flowers, libations, etc.). For only an ensouled person would already have, in the face of death, the non-perceptual intuition of soul necessary to recognize and affirm the contradiction in the first place. An unsouled person, if such there be, could signify death, but would have no reason to contradict it.

*

The Soul 137

This suggests another way to approach the soul—through language. Thoughts which picture or analogize sensations can be called 'impressions' And sensations which picture or analogize thoughts can be called 'expressions.' Impressions picture or analogize sensations which are not themselves pictures or analogies of thoughts; and expressions picture or analogize thoughts which are not themselves pictures or analogies of sensations. A thought is an impression for me only if I recognize it as a picture or analog of a sensation. A sensation is an expression for me only if I recognize it as a picture or analog of a thought. For example, if a thought of a pain I felt a year ago is an impression, that is, a picture or analog of the sensation of a year ago, it is because it displays for me the same forms as did that sensation. And if the first four tones of Beethoven's *Fifth Symphony* constitute an expression, that is, a picture or analog of a thought, it is because they display for me the same forms as does some thought.

Thoughts, being contingent to sensations, cannot be reproduced in sensation, but what it is that thoughts combine to display can be represented by combinations of sensations (expressions). And sensations, being contingent to thoughts, cannot be reproduced in thought, but what it is that sensations combine to display can be represented by combinations of thoughts (impressions). And combinations of thoughts can be represented publicly as expressions. This is the secret of the power of language. Language is the most flexible, succinct, and extensive mode of expression because it utilizes thoughts to transform sensations.

Insofar as combinations of thoughts are spontaneous and effortless, their capacity as representational vehicles is unlimited. I can represent in thought virtually any forms displayed by sensations. But since combinations of sensations are never spontaneous and effortless, their capacity as representational vehicles is compromised. I cannot, without some degree of labor, or dissipation of energy, represent in sensation forms represented in thought. An impression such as a memory is instant and energy-free (recall your mother's face); an expression, on the other hand, is a task for someone (draw your mother's face). To recognize others is to recognize that they are like myself. It is to recognize one's private thinking self being made public by someone else in sensation. To fail to recognize an expression as an expression is to fail to see something sensible as a representation of something thought. And to fail to see something sensible as a representation of something thought is to fail to recognize the expression of a person.

I suggested, in the chapter on language, that the soul is a value, an awareness arising out of the comparison of the perceptions given in consciousness and our consciousness of ourselves as distinct from those perceptions. The question is: when do we accept public perceptual evaluations of soul from other sources? If my dog learnt Morse code and sent me messages, I would have to recognize in him a power of expression that would make him a person. Similarly, if a machine, say a robot or computer, did the same, we should be tempted to recognize it—as Alan Turing suggested—as a person. Since we ourselves are animals that are persons, it is not so far-fetched that other animals might also be persons. It is also possible that there might be machines that are persons. But the latter seems far less likely as long as non-physical thoughts remain as mysteriously divorced from sensations as we have seen them to be.

A machine can be programmed to display activity in response to stimuli, to make choices, and even to replicate itself. It might even be programed to speak a language, or to appear to do so to all intents and purposes. But no machine can be programed with the capacity for self-consciousness. We do not even know how to begin to program a machine to have thoughts, so we cannot even begin to make a person, let alone a soul. In our machine building, we are limited to working with sensations: hence the temptation to fall into behavioristic psychology, reducing not only thought but consciousness to sensation.

We are tempted to attribute consciousness or soul to animals (even without any evidence that they have thoughts) because they are so expressive of emotion and will and share so much of our own biological structure. We are more inclined to do so the more similar they are to us. The emotion and will they display are persuasive bridges to and from the soul. Machines, on the other hand, generally fail to persuade in this way. The idea that machines might be programed to speak has been their strongest promise of similarity, yet even this need show no more than the ingenuity of the programmers. Even a machine that passed Turing's test need not satisfy us. It would be like being fooled at a magic show, or by a computerized voice on the telephone. We would know the machine was made by someone, and it would be sufficient and appropriate to attribute whatever soul it seemed to demonstrate to its creator, not to the machine.

Any machine simulating human behavior at any level cannot remotely be regarded as being ensouled or aware as long as no appeal to soul or awareness is necessary to make it understood. Yet of course that is the whole point of the behaviorist enterprise. The behaviorist claim—that awareness can be reduced to sensation—can be sustained, however, only at the cost of making awareness a meaningless term. I can recognize a machine as a soul, but only by denying what we mean by soul and concluding, in effect, that I myself am no more than a machine.

*

We are souls distinct from but mixed with various perceptions. What I seek as a soul from my perceptions is satisfaction, and the will is the means to that end. The will is normally guided by emotion (the effects of perceptions on the soul) registered in desire and aversion. I can exercise the will without desire or aversion, either indifferently or for its own sake. I also seek satisfaction from other souls, and I can use the will to act in perception so as to attract other souls. The satisfaction I seek from them is not the perceptual satisfaction of mind and body, but the satisfaction of mutual recognition and appreciation beyond mind and body we call friendship and love. I can also exercise the will for its own sake, rather than to attract perceptions and souls. But it makes sense to do so only on the belief that the will can be satisfied only by itself, only by further willing, which in turn demands even further willing, and so on endlessly. This regress makes it plain that the will cannot be satisfied by itself. The closest one can come to willing indifferently is to do so to make the point of being able to do so (the exception that proves the rule).

The will can be satisfied in perception only if it is motivated by desire, that is, by perceptions affecting the soul. Perceptions strike us in many ways, and we find ourselves searching and sifting the perceptions of our experience for satisfaction. Perceptual satisfaction is not simply the end of desire (since desire can end without satisfaction). It is the end of desire in some perception. To say that satisfaction is possible in perception is to say that perceptions can absorb the will. The harnessing of the will to the unfolding of a perception appropriate to the scope of the will is, assuming the intrinsic merit of the perception, the ultimate happiness we can find in perception.

Perceptual desire is possible only in the absence of a desirable perception of which one is reminded by some other perception which represents or is related to it. Our perceptual desires are primarily preoccupied with our sensations since it is the difficulty in retrieving sensations (by comparison with thoughts) that compounds the work of the will and intensifies desire. Sensible perceptions are difficult to retrieve because energy must be expended to do so. Thoughts too are sometimes difficult to retrieve; they can be blocked, and our ensuing frustration may manifest itself in a physical expenditure of energy. But, as we have seen, such blocks are located in some physical condition of thought, and not in thought itself.

Thoughts *per se* remain open to effortless substitution for one another. This very quality of thought makes the impressions we hold of absent sensations the occasion to desire those sensations. Thoughts in this way magnify the desire for sensations already occasioned by the labor required to achieve them (even as they help to simplify that labor). But to satisfy our perceptual desires we must, usually with the guidance of thought, act in the sensible world. Our perceptual satisfaction, or personal happiness, depends upon our success in achieving the physical perceptions that stir our will and demand its absorption. The mind can satisfy itself, fulfill its own wishes in fantasy, easily enough (unless it is neurotically or psychotically obsessed). Our thoughts fail to satisfy us only insofar as they represent sensations we desire. It is the body, and the public world of sensation given to us through the body, that consistently burdens us. The most pressing needs of the body—for food and drink, shelter, and sex—are familiar enough, as are the more subtle needs that arise when these are satisfied. We want, as much as anything else in perception, to eliminate unwanted labor, to gain the effortlessness in sensation that we enjoy in thought. This is inherent in every perceptual desire. It is part of every perceptual desire that it should cease to be. Not that it should be denied, or repressed, but that it should be discharged in satisfaction.

The Soul

The attractive power of a perception is rooted in the forms that perception displays. We want to appropriate the perceptions we desire in order to incorporate in ourselves their forms, or some more ineffable residue thereof. We want to command their presence so as to transform ourselves as persons. Just how we incorporate a perception depends on our own constitution (the special thoughts and sensations that make us just the persons we are, as well as the larger perceptions of which, as persons, we are parts). It also depends on the constitution of the desired perception (on its parts and on the wholes to which it belongs). Since the focus of perceptual desire is mainly on certain sensations, incorporating those sensations means actually possessing, or sensing, them. The sensation of my desire must be a sight I want to see, a sound I want to hear, a touch I want to feel, a smell I want to smell, or a taste I want to taste—or a combination of any or all of these. I search through desire for forms displayed in certain sights, sounds, etc., and in their combination. The power of such forms, their relative attractiveness, is itself inexplicable. It is simply given.

But the satisfaction of a perceptual desire is also an activity—the will must be consumed in the utilization of the desired perception. Once it is before us, we do not passively confront a perception we desire. We consume it. We proceed to put that perception to use, exploiting its internal and external relations. It is one thing to exercise the will to obtain the perception we desire (in anticipation of it); it is another thing to exercise the will in the consumption of that perception. If I succeed in obtaining possession of a perception I desire—say, a physical object—only then can I proceed to utilize it. If the physical object is an apple, I proceed to examine it: I consider the situation in which it appears, the whole or wholes of which it is a part (the tree upon which it hangs, the store shelf upon which it rests, etc.). I pick the apple, carry it about, bring it home, eat it, and so on. And in the process, insofar as I peel it, slice it, squeeze it, chew it, digest it, and so on, I exploit its internal as well as external relations.

Perceptual satisfaction is the discharge of the will in the consumption of a desired perception. The satisfaction of desire includes, but is not reduced to, the alleviation of the direct needs of the body. These needs—hunger, thirst, sex, warmth, etc.—are themselves tensions, that is, accumulations of undischarged will. They are satisfied only by an appropriate perception, one which can absorb the accumulated will in question. Hunger, thirst, etc., are not themselves desires, but tensions of the will. They are joined by desire only when a perception able to absorb them is represented. We desire food and water and the bodies of others, not hunger and thirst and sex. And, of course, representations of perceptions attractive to the will can stimulate it even when it is not tensed-up or accumulated. I might not be hungry, but the appearance of good food, or even the representation of it, can stimulate my interest. None of this is to say that satisfaction is necessarily good for us. The perceptions we seek out for our satisfaction may be harmful. I may desire to put butter on my bread, but the cholesterol in the butter may harm my body's cardiovascular system. Or I may become a masochist and seek sexual satisfaction through inflicting harm on my body. The value of a perception need not have anything to do with whether or not we desire that perception. Moreover, many of our desires cannot be satisfied, leaving us frustrated. And chronic frustration leads to resentment, to alienation and anger, the opposites of satisfaction.

We also seek non-perceptual satisfactions. Such satisfactions lie not in perception but in the mutual recognition of souls. Insofar as I intuit my own soul, I desire the recognition and esteem of other souls, and I solicit it by offering them, among other things, my recognition and esteem. Sometimes one soul recognizes another instantly and thoroughly, sometimes gradually; sometimes recognition is mutual; sometimes not. There are perhaps as many possibilities of recognition as there are souls. Insofar as two souls attracted to one another succeed in mutual recognition, they gain in mutual respect, and their mutual recognition and esteem grows into friendship, and ultimately love. Friendship and love are perhaps our deepest emotions, those which 'color' the soul most completely.

Sometimes, however, souls—distracted by solipsistic and behavioristic attachments—repulse rather than attract, irritate rather than soothe. A soul which confuses itself with perception—solipsistically or behavioristically (or humanistically)—sees itself not as a soul but as a thought or a sensation, a mind or a body, (or a person). Recognition of self and others is displaced onto perceptions. Although it denies itself and others, such a soul blunders on, seeking satisfaction in perception. Only the distinction of the soul from perception allows for the self and mutual recognition of souls as souls. It also allows for the undistorted recognition of thoughts and sensations as perceptions distinct from ourselves, and for an appreciation of the proper role of perception as the mediator of souls.

The unconditional freedom of the private world of thought reflects its function as a vehicle of omnipotent but lonely perceptual self-realization. The recalcitrant vastness of the public world of sensation reflects its function as an endless stage for numberless bodies. The paradoxical conjunction of thoughts and sensations in persons makes possible the intuition and mutual recognition of souls as other than perceptions. We need both thoughts and sensations to discover that we are souls in the company of other souls for whom thoughts and sensations, and even personalities, are finally means and not ends. It may be the stubborn incompleteness of solipsism and behaviorism, the mutual inability of either to absorb the other, and our disappointments with the satisfactions they offer, that disposes us to the intuition of the soul. The liberation of soul from perception appears to be the precondition of ultimate happiness, or enlightenment. But souls are long conditioned by their solipsistic and behavioristic entanglements, and any self-and-other awareness of souls may be temporary and incomplete. The evolution of the soul, of awareness, if our short experience is any guide, may even require more than one lifetime.

*

In the modern world the notion of the soul is banished as a superstition, a myth. My defense of the soul aligns me with religious traditionalists (Christians, Jews, Muslims, Hindus, classical pagans, African animists, and many others) who admit a soul. But I cannot accept their views insofar as each of them can be shown to commit the error of attempting somehow to represent the soul in perception. Any such representation—which becomes a litmus test of the faith—necessarily confuses souls with perceptions. And this confusion is the slippery slope leading to solipsism and behaviorism where the soul is denied by judging all experience according to the standards of perception. Solipsism and behaviorism leave no place for the soul. The only reality for them is the reality of perception.

The traditional religions are half-way houses to solipsism and behaviorism, to denying the soul. They attempt to capture the soul in two ways: by appeal to some privileged perception (like the life of Jesus, or the Buddha), or to some pattern of perceptions (like the argument from design). These appeals, one to perceptual archetypes artistically rendered, and the other to relational paradigms scientifically established, are appeals to the perceptual-world of representation. But the soul is not a matter of perception, and no overt gesture, defining ritualistic act, or dogmatic abstract formulation can stand as a criterion of the soul. The soul cannot be artistically rendered or scientifically established. It is given to each of us, directly but ineffably, as an intuited value. Each of us is in essence a mysterious soul somehow aware of perceptions—thoughts and sensations (minds and bodies), persons, and cultures—and willfully inspired and emotionally affected by these perceptions. Each of us is also, at best, aware of ourselves (and others) as a soul, with will and emotion, and it is this self-awareness that mysteriously points us beyond what we are as persons.

Bibliography

Abbott, Edwin A. *Flatland: A Romance of Many Dimensions.* New York: Barnes and Noble, 1963.

Adams, Raymond D. and Victor, Maurice. *Principles of Neurology.* New York: McGraw-Hill Book Co., 1977.

Ancilla to the Pre-Socratic Philosophers: A Complete Translation of the Fragments in Diel's Fragmente der Vorsokratiker. Trans. Kathleen Freeman. Cambridge: Harvard University Press, 1966.

Aristotle. *The Basic Works of Aristotle.* Richard McKeon, ed. New York: Random House, 1941.

Ayer, A. J. *Language, Truth and Logic.* New York: Dover Publications, n.d.

Bateson, Gregory. *Steps to an Ecology of Mind.* New York: Ballatine Books, 1972.

Bergson, Henri. *Creative Evolution.* Trans. by Arthur Mitchell. New York: Modern Library, 1944.

Berkeley, George. *The Works of George Berkeley, Bishop of Cloyne.* 5 vols. A. A. Luce and T. E. Jessop, Eds. London: Thomas Nelson and Sons, 1967.

Bochenski, J. M. *The Methods of Contemporary Thought.* Trans. Peter Caws. New York: Harper and Row, 1968.

Bohm, David. *Wholeness and the Implicate Order.* London: Routledge & Kegan Paul, 1980.

The Book of the Dead. The Papyrus of Ani in the British Museum. The Egyptian Text with Interlinear Transliteration and Translation, a Running Translation, Introduction, etc., by E.A. Wallis Budge. New York: Dover Publications, Inc., 1967.

Bram, Marvin. *On the Crisis of Intellection.* Ann Arbor: University Microfilms, 1973.

Brown, Norman O. *Life Against Death: The Psychoanalytical Meaning of History.* Middletown, Conn.: Wesleyan University Press, 1959.

_____. *Love's Body.* New York: Random House, 1966.

Buchler, Justus. *Metaphysics of Natural Complexes.* New York: Columbia University Press, 1966.

Budge, E. A. Wallis. *Osiris and the Egyptian Resurrection.* 2 vols. New York: Dover Publications, 1911.

Castaneda, Carlos. *The Eagle's Gift.* New York: Simon and Shuster, 1981.

Chadwick, John. *The Decipherment of Linear B.* Cambridge, U.K.: Cambridge University Press, 1970.

Chuang Tzu. *The Complete Works of Chuang Tzu.* Trans. Burton Watson. New York: Columbia University Press, 1968.

Churchland, Patricia Smith. *Neurophilosophy: Towards a Unified Science of the Mind/Brain.* Cambridge, Mass.: MIT Press, 1990.

Churchland, Paul M. *Matter and Consciousness: A Contemporary Introduction to the Philosophy of Mind.* rev. ed. Cambridge, Mass.: MIT Press, 1988.

Collingwood, R. G. *An Essay on Metaphysics.* Chicago: Henry Regnery Company, 1972.

_____. *The Idea of History.* London: Oxford University Press, 1956.

Copi, Irving M. *Introduction to Logic.* 2nd ed. New York: Macmillan, 1961.

Crick, Francis and Koch, Christof. "The Problem of Consciousness" in *Scientific American.* Sept. 1992.

Dennett, Daniel C. *Brainstorms: Philosophical Essays on Mind and Psychology.* Bradford Books, 1978.

Derrida, Jacques. *Of Grammatology.* Trans. Gayatri Chakravorty Spivak. Baltimore: Johns Hopkins University Press, 1976.

Descartes, Rene. *The Philosophical Works of Descartes.* 2 vols. Trans. Haldane and Ross. Cambridge: Cambridge University Press. 1967.

Deussen, Paul. *The System of the Vedanta.* New York: Dover Publications, 1973.

Eccles, John C. *The Human Mystery.* Berlin: Springer International. 1979.

_____. *The Understanding of the Brain.* New York: McGraw-Hill Book Company, 1973.

Eckhart, Meister. *Meister Eckhart: A Modern Translation.* Trans. by Raymond Bernard Blakney. New York: Harper and Row, 1941.

Eliade, Mircea. *The Myth of the Eternal Return, or Cosmos and History.* Trans. Willard R. Trask. New York: Princeton University Press, 1954.

Empiricus, Sextus. *Outlines of Pyrrhonism.* Trans. by R. G. Bury. Buffalo, N.Y.: Prometheus Books, 1990.

Engelmann, Paul. *Letters from Ludwig Wittgenstein, with a Memoir.* New York: Horizon Press, 1968.

Euclid. *The Thirteen Books of Euclid's Elements.* 3 vols. Trans. by Sir Thomas L. Heath. New York: Dover Publications, 1956.

Feyerabend, Paul. *Against Method.* London: Verso, 1978.

Flew, Anthony. "Immortality" in *The Encyclopedia of Philosophy.* vol. 4. Ed. by Paul Edwards. New York: Macmillan Publishing Co. Inc., and The Free Press, 1967.

Foucault, Michel. *The Archaeology of Knowlege.* Trans. A. M. Sheridan Smith. New York: Pantheon Books, 1972.

Frankfort, Henri, et. al. *The Intellectual Adventure of Ancient Man.* Chicago: University of Chicago Press, 1946.

Frege, Gottlob. *Translations from the Philosophical Writrings of Gottlob Frege.* Trans. by Peter Geach and Max Black. Oxford: Basil Blackwell, 1970.

Freud, Sigmund. *A General Introduction to Psychoanalysis.* Trans. by Joan Riviere. New York: Simon and Schuster, 1935.

_____. *The Interpretation of Dreams.* Trans. by James Strachey. New York: Avon Books, 1965.

Gordon, Cyrus H. *Forgotten Scripts: Their Ongoing Discovery and Decipherment.* Revised and enlarged ed. New York: Basic Books, Inc., 1968.

Havelock, Eric A. *Preface to Plato.* Oxford: Basil Blackwell, 1963.

Hegel, G. W. F. *Phenomenology of Spirit.* Trans. by A. V. Miller. Oxford: Oxford University Press, 1979.

⎯⎯⎯⎯. *The Philosophy of History.* Trans. J. Sibree. New York: Dover Publications, Inc., 1956.

Heidegger, Martin. *Being and Time.* Trans. by J. Macquarrie and E. Robinson. New York: Harper & Row, 1962.

⎯⎯⎯⎯. *What is a Thing?* Trans. W. B. Barton, Jr. and Vera Deutsch. Chicago: Henry Regnery Co., 1967.

Heisenberg, Werner. *Physics and Philosophy: The Revolution in Modern Science.* New York: Harper and Row, 1958.

Holton, Gerald and Roller, Duane. *Foundations of Modern Physical Science.* Reading, MA: Addison-Wesley Publishing, 1958.

Horkheimer, Max. *Eclipse of Reason.* New York: Seabury Press, 1947.

Huizinga, Johan. *The Waning of the Middle Ages.* Trans. by F. Hopman. Garden City, NJ: Doubleday Anchor, 1954.

Jaynes, Julian. *The Origin of Consciousness in the Breakdown of the Bicameral Mind.* Boston: Houghton Mifflin, 1976.

Joyce, James. *Finnegans Wake.* New York: The Viking Press, 1959.

Kant, Immanuel. *Critique of Judgment.* Trans J. H. Bernard. New York: Hafner Publishing Co., 1966.

⎯⎯⎯⎯. *Critique of Practical Reason.* Trans. by Lewis White Beck. Indianapolis: Bobbs-Merrill, 1956.

⎯⎯⎯⎯. *Critique of Pure Reason.* Trans. by Norman Kemp Smith. New York: St. Martin's Press, 1965.

Koestler, Arthur. *The Ghost in the Machine.* Chicago: Henry Regnery Co., 1967.

Bibliography

Kojeve, Alexandre. *Introduction to the Reading of Hegel.* Trans. James H. Nichols, Jr. New York: Basic Books, Inc., 1969.

Kuhn, Thomas S. *The Structure of Scientific Revolutions.* Chicago: University of Chicago Press, 1962.

Kuzminski, Adrian. "Archetypes and Paradigms" in *History and Theory.* vol. xxv, no. 3. 1986.

_____. *The Languages of the World: The Dilemmans of Rationalist Thought and the Linguistic Metaphysics of George Berkeley.* Ann Arbor: University Microfilms, 1973.

_____. "The Paradox of Historical Knowledge" in *History and Theory*, vol. xii, no. 3. 1973.

_____. "Wittgenstein's Mystical Realism" in *The Yale Review.* vol. lxviii, no. 4. Summer, 1979.

LaBerge, Stephen. *Lucid Dreaming.* New York: Ballantine Books, 1985.

Laertius, Diogenes. *Lives of the Philosophers.* Trans. by A. Robert Caponigri. Chicago: Henry Regnery, 1969.

Lao Tzu. *Tao te Ching.* Trans. D. C. Lau. Baltimore: Penguin Books, 1963.

Leibniz, Gottfried Wilhelm von. *Monadology and other Philosophical Essays.* Trans. Paul Schrecker. Indianapolis: Bobb-Merrill Co., 1965.

Levi-Strauss, Claude. Anonymous trans. *The Savage Mind.* London: Weidenfeld and Nicolson, 1966.

Locke, John. *An Essay Concerning Human Understanding.* 2 vols. Alexander Campbell Fraser, ed. New York: Dover Publications, 1959.

Luckert, Karl W. *Egyptian Light and Hebrew Fire: Theological and Philosophical Roots of Christendom in Evolutionary Perspective.* Albany: SUNY Press, 1991.

Luria, A. R. *The Mind of a Menemonist: A Little Book about a Vast Memory.* Trans. by Lynn Solotaroff. Chicago: Henry Regnery Co., 1968.

Malcolm, Norman. *Ludwig Wittgenstein: A Memoir.* With a Biographical Sketch by George Henrik von Wright. London: Oxford University Press, 1958.

Mandelbaum, Maurice. *History, Man, and Reason*. Baltimore: John Hopkins University Press, 1971.

Mannheim, Karl. *Ideology and Utopia: An Introduction to the Sociology of Knowledge*. Trans. by Louis Wirth and Edward Shils. New York: Harcourt, Brace and World, 1936.

Marcuse, Herbert. *One-Dimensional Man: Studies in the Ideology of Advanced Industrial Society*. Boston: Beacon Press, 1967.

Marshack, Alexander. *The Roots of Civilization: The Cognitive Beginnings of Man's First Art, Symbol and Notation*. New York: McGraw-Hill Book Company, 1972.

Marx, Karl. *Capital: A Critique of Political Economy*. vol 1. Trans. by Samuel Moore and Edward Aveling. New York: International Publishers, 1967.

Marx, Karl and Engels, Frederick. *The German Ideology*. Trans. by C. J. Arthur. New York: International Publishers, 1970.

Melzack, Ronald. 'Phantom Limbs', in *Scientific American,* April, 1992.

Merleau-Ponty, M. *Phemenology of Perception*. Trans. by Colin Smith. London: Routledge and Kegan Paul, 1965.

Monk, Ray. *Ludwig Wittgenstein: The Duty of Genius*. London: Penguin, 1990.

Monroe, Robert A. *Journeys Out of the Body*. New York: Doubleday, 1971.

Moore, A. W. *The Infinite*. London: Routledge, 1990.

Moore, G. E. *Principia Ethica*. Cambridge, U.K.: Cambridge University Press, 1959.

Moravec, Hans. *Mind Children: The Future of Robot and Human Intelligence*. Cambridge, MA: Harvard University Press, 1988.

Nagel, Ernest and Newman, James R. *Godel's Proof*. New York: New York University Press, 1968.

The New English Bible. Sandmel, Suggs, and Tkacik, eds. New York: Oxford University Press, 1976.

Bibliography

Nietzsche, Friedrich. *Beyond Good and Evil: Prelude to a Philosophy of the Future.* Trans. Walter Kaufmann. New York: Vintage Books, 1966.

_____. *The Birth of Tragedy and The Geneology of Morals.* Trans. Francis Golffing. Garden City, N.J.: Doubleday & Co., 1956.

_____. *The Will to Power.* Trans. W. Kaufmann and R. J. Hollingdale. New York: Vintage Books, 1967.

Onians, R. B. *The Origins of European Thought: About the Body, the Mind, the Soul, the World, Time, and Fate.* Cambridge, U.K.: Cambridge University Press, 1988.

Pepper, Stephen C. *World Hypotheses: A Study in Evidence.* Berkeley, Calif.: University of California Press, 1948.

Plato. *The Collected Dialogues of Plato.* Edith Hamilton and Huntington Cairns, eds. New York: Bollingen Foundation and Random House, 1963.

Plotinus. *The Enneads.* Trans. Stephen MacKenna. London: Penguin, 1991.

Popkin, Richard H. *The History of Scepticism: From Erasmus to Descartes.* Revised ed. New York: Harper and Row, 1964.

Popper, Karl R. *The Poverty of Historicism.* New York: Harper Torchbooks, 1957.

Pseudo-Dionysius. *Pseudo-Dionyusius: The Complete Works.* Luibheid, Rorem, Roques, Pelikan, et. al. New York: Paulist Press, 1987.

Quine, Willard Van Orman. *From a Logical Point of View.* New York: Harper Torchbooks, 1963.

_____. *Word and Object.* Cambridge, Mass.: MIT Press, 1960.

Rorty, Richard. *Philosophy and the Mirror of Nature.* Princeton, N.J.: Princeton University Press, 1979.

Rundle Clark, R. T. *Myth and Symbol in Ancient Egypt.* London: Thames and Husdon, Ltd., 1959.

Russell, Bertrand. *Logic and Knowledge: Essays 1901-1950.* Robert C. Marsh, ed. London: George Allen & Unwin, 1956.

_____. *Principles of Mathematics*. New York: W. W. Norton, n.d.

Ryle, Gilbert. *The Concept of Mind*. New York: Barnes and Noble, 1949.

Searle, John. *Minds, Brains, and Science*. Cambridge: Harvard University Press, 1984.

Sohn-Rethel, Alfred. *Intellectual and Manuel Labor: A Critique of Epistemology*. London: Macmillan Press Ltd., 1978.

Spinoza, Baruch. *The Ethics and Selected Letters*. Trans. Samuel Shirley. Indianapolis: Hackett Publishing Co., 1982.

Stevens, Jay. *Storming Heaven: LSD and the American Dream*. New York: The Atlantic Monthly Press, 1967.

Swinburne, Richard. *The Evolution of the Soul*. Oxford: Clarendon Press, 1986.

Thompson, Richard L. *Mechanistic and Non-Mechanistic Science: An Investigation into the Nature of Consciousness and Form*. Los Angeles: The Bhaktivedanta Book Trust, 1981.

The Tibetan Book of the Dead, Or the After-Death Experiences on the Bardo Plane, according to Lama Kazi Dawa-Samdup's English Rendering, compiled and edited by W.Y. Evans-Wentz. London: Oxford University Press, 1969.

Turbayne, Colin M. *The Myth of Metaphor*. Rev. ed. Columbia, S.C.: University of South Carolina Press, 1970.

Snell, Bruno. *The Discovery of the Mind: The Greek Origins of European Thought*. New York: Harper and Row, 1960.

Vico, Giambattista. *The New Science of Giambattista Vico*. Trans. by Bergin and Fisch. Ithaca: Cornell University Press, 1968.

Weil, Andrew. *The Natural Mind: An Investigation of Drugs and the Higher Consciousness*. Boston: Houghton Mifflin, 1972.

Whitehead, Alfred North. *Process and Reality*. Corrected ed. Griffin and Sherburne, eds. New York: The Free Press, 1978.

Bibliography

Wittgenstein, Ludwig. *On Certainty.* Trans. Denis Paul and G. E. M. Anscombe. German and English. New York: Harper and Row, 1972.

_____. *Philosophical Investigations.* Trans. G. E. M. Anscombe. 3rd ed. German and English. New York: Macmillan Co., 1958.

_____. *Tractatus Logico-Philosophicus.* Trans. by D. F. Pears and B. F. McGuinness. German and English. London: Routledge & Kegan Paul, 1961.

_____. *Remarks on the Foundations of Mathematics.* G. E. M. Ansconbe. German and English. Cambridge, Mass.: MIT Press, 1956.

Woolley, Benjamin. *Virtual Worlds: A Journey in Hype and Hyperreality.* Oxford: Blackwell, 1992.

Yates, Frances A. *The Art of Memory.* Chicago: University of Chicago Press, 1966.

Yohananda, Paramahausa. *Autobiography of a Yogi.* Los Angeles: Self-Realization Fellowship, 1946.

_____. *Man's Eternal Quest.* Los Angeles: Self-Realization Fellowship, 1976.

Zimmer, Heinrich. *Philosophies of India.* Joseph Campbell, ed. New York: Bolligen Foundation, and Princeton: Princeton University Press, 1951.

Index

A

Academy, ancient, 82
African animists, 143
Alternate realities, 59
Americans
    culture of, 129
animals, 135–136
Artois, 74
Atlantis, 44

B

Bach, J. S.
    fugue, 92, 95
Beethoven, Ludwig von
    Fifth Symphony, 137
Berkeley, George, 129
    *A Treatise Concerning the
    Principles of Human
    Knowledge*, 46–47
Bernardino of Siena, 68
Bible, 68, 124
Bohr, Niels, 5
brain, 51, 53, 64, 134
    waves, 66
Buddha, 68, 144
Buddhism, 133
Burgundy, House of, 74

C

Catholic mass. *See* Mass,
    Catholic
Chastellain, 74
Chinese
    Mandarin, 111
Christ. *See* Jesus
Christianity, 81, 83, 143
Civil War, 30
Complementarity,
    principle of, 5

D

Democritus, 81
Dickens, Charles, 83
Dionysius, 82
drugs, 53, 59, 133, 134

E

Eccles, John C.
    The Human Mystery, 134
Egypt, 81
Einstein, Albert, 72
English
    alphabet, 96, 98
    language, 109
Enlightenment, 81, 83
Epicurus, 81

F

French Revolution, 81
Freud, Sigmund, 72
Froissart, 74

G

God, 65, 123
Greeks, ancient, 78, 81, 127

H

Hainout, 74
Heisenberg, Werner, 6
Hinduism, 82
Hindus, 60, 143
Holy Roman Empire, 74
homo sapiens, 58
Huizinga, Johan, 74
The Waning of the Middle Ages, 68
human beings, 2

I

indeterminacy, principle of, 6
irony, 123, 124
Islam, 81, 143

J

Jesus Christ,
    68, 80, 82, 83, 144
Judaism, 82, 143

K

Kaballah, 60
Koran, 68

L

Lincoln, Abraham, 38
Lucretius, 81
Lycium, ancient, 82

M

Mandarin Chinese. *See* Chinese: Mandarin
Marshack, Alexander 81
Mass, Catholic, 83
mathematical logic, 23
Mayan bars and dots, 38
meditation
    meditative techniques, 127
Mesopotamia, 81
metaphor, 122, 124, 124–125
Mexico, 44
Molinet, 74
Mondrian, 35
Morse code, 138
Muslims. *See* Islam

N

Nationalism, 83
Neanderthals, 136
Newton, Isaac, 72
Newtonian mechanics, 80
North Dakota, 36
numbers, whole, 100
numerals, Arabic, 38

O

out-of-body experiences, 134
out-of-the-body experiences, 59

P

paganism, 81, 143
Paris, 27
Planck, Max, 6
Planck's constant, 6

Q

quantum physics, 6, 55

R

racism, 83
Renaissance, 81
Roman letters, 38
Romans, 81, 127

S

Sears Roebuck
  catalog, 83
Shintoism, 82
Socrates, 133
Sufis, 60
Suso, Henry, 68

T

Turing, Alan, 138

U

U. S. in World War I. *See*
  World War I: U.S. entry

V

virtual reality, 133, 134

W

West Virginia, 36
Western culture, 82
Wittgenstein, Ludwig, 73
  Remarks on the Foundation of
  Mathematics, 102–103
World War I
  United State entry into, 112

Z

Zeus, 90

Revisioning Philosophy

The series seeks innovative and explorative thought in the foundation, aim, and objectives of philosophy. Preference will be given to approaches to world philosophy and to the repositioning of traditional viewpoints. New understandings of knowledge and being in the history of philosophy will be considered. Works may take the form of monographs, collected essays, and translations which demonstrate the imaginative flair of examining foundational questions.

The series editor is:

David Appelbaum
Department of Philosophy
The College at New Paltz
New Paltz, NY 12561